Good Girl
Fine Girl
Charming Girl

Deborah McFatter
Bonnie Cordova
Edna Teller

Copyright © 2019
Deborah McFatter, Bonnie Cordova,
Edna Teller

All rights reserved.

ISBN: 9781070182452

Contents

A Foreword from the Editor 1

Deborah Is A Good Girl 6

Bonnie Is A Fine Girl 48

Edna Is A Charming Girl 88

A Foreword from the Editor

They say they met in an improv class in Los Feliz, California, in 2013, and that they became friends soon after, sharing an uncanny spirit of introspection, remembrance, sensitivity, humor, and appreciation of creativity.

I call bullshit.

The three women who authored this memoir—Debbi, Edna, and Bonnie—must have known each other much longer than that. Triplets, from the same womb, because I've read this book. I edited it, actually, and the lives they experienced are too similar. They don't express themselves the same way, at all, but they each share the same bizarre sense of humor, the same messy childhood, the same insecurities. The same problems with assholes. But also, the same hope for a better life, a better environment. Better politics.

Whatever force brought these three together, it must have been from a divine power. I don't care if you're Atheist, or Christian, or Jewish, or Jew-theist. Something brought these women together and ordered them to start a writing circle, so they could grace us with snippets of their lives, to bring us three colorful characters in a sea of gray. To wake us up, slap us with a slice of pizza, and say, You'll always have to deal with some jerk at some point in your life. The best thing you can do is continue to be yourself, don't let those insecurities seep too deeply inside of you because, well, we all go through bad times that test us. The difference is how quickly you can pick yourself back up.

Sewn together with the hem of an A-line dress splattered in spaghetti sauce, this collection of memories presents the reader with a profound image of growing up in the '50s and '60s, of getting married amid rocky circumstances, and of being a woman during those times. At times it reveals a more personal look at the sexism then (as opposed to the sexism now), as well as the mindset of women and how they coped with that nonsense. It is about body image, about insecurity, about getting over some of that insecurity but always living with it, about shitty husbands, and about pretty good ones, and sometimes just about ice cream.

I see this book as an art gallery, three painters splashing their life experiences onto each page, employing their own style. At times it is expressionistic, sometimes socially oriented, and, often, absurd. And, like an art gallery with a central theme but exhibiting various styles, this collection provides dimension where there was none, a deeper understanding, a more complete picture of that theme.

For example, Debbi's writing often goes straight to memories that weren't always kind to her, to explain (to herself as well as the audience) why she is who she is today. Explanations for her fears, for those lingering pains that we are all trying to leave behind. A lot of fear of being punished. Her work is a self-portrait baring all the blemishes, all the imperfections. Her work is much like that of Edvard Munch, an expressionist who is known for creating revealing pieces, nudes, "The Scream". He, too, bares all, despite his own insecurities, in an effort to express why he is who he is. She has fashioned herself the "Good Girl", not because of her ceaseless altruism (as if!), but because of the heap of expectations her evangelical upbringing placed on her throughout her life.

Edna's work has an element of this as well, but her lines are starker, her prose is more defined. She is the Inventor, trying to explain why her automaton functions the way it does today. The way this is expressed is revealing, provocative at times, telling of the mid-twentieth century, and her journalistic style of writing is clear and feels somewhat polished. Edna writes like Rembrandt painted, in that she does not leave any details out. Like Debbi, Edna's writing is a self-portrait but with unwavering lines. Edna is the self-decreed "Charming Girl", in that she takes no shit from others.

Bonnie's approach differs a bit more than the others, in that she doesn't always use her past to directly explain how she feels today, or why she is where she is. She just remembers something that sparks her imagination and then flings it onto the page, like Jackson Pollock. This wilder approach allows the reader to use their imagination a bit more, and, paradoxically, makes it easier for the audience to relate their own experiences with hers. The memories she writes about are never offered explanation, rather they're a splatter of feelings, thoughts, ideas. In Bonnie's words, she's the "Fine Girl", the girl who was overlooked, who did just fine, but not much else. This could not be further from the truth. Like the other two, she's a f#$%@ing rock star.

    I hope you enjoy the work presented here by these three wonderful women. Better yet—I hope these pieces dig deep inside of you, tear out your pumpkin guts, those feelings of guilt, those insecurities that you have been mewling over your whole life. Know that there are at least three women holding in much heftier (and more bizarre-looking) baggage. And they're sharing it with you in the hopes that you'll help carry this baggage, because, dammit, yet again their gate just had to be all the way on the other side of the airport. Typical goddamn luck.

Peter Gaskin, Editor.

Deborah Is A Good Girl

For Family—who were before me, are with me, and come after me—
you are my story.

In early 2017, four years after we parted ways, Bonnie, Edna, and I held a mini-reunion at Union Station in Los Angeles. Like many Americans at that point, we were all anxious about what lay ahead for our democracy. At one point in our lunch, at a quaint Mexican restaurant on Olvera Street, we began to improvise a song expressing our confusion over the current state of affairs in American politics. There was a lot of guffawing at ourselves, and we even touched on writing some songs as therapy for our angst. Bonnie has a dog named Frannie and a cat, Harley. Somehow, we glommed onto "Frannie and the Cat" as a catchy name for our little band.

The collective songwriting went nowhere. In 2018, Bonnie suggested that we do a daily writing exercise with prompts that she would send us by email. What started as a ten-minute practice soon became so satisfying and challenging that we started writing for more than ten minutes. Before long we realized that what each of us was writing individually had common themes, memories of what it was like growing up female in the 1950s and 1960s, even though we came from disparate homes.

Frannie and the Cat stuck for our little trio.

She Laughed Last

She was very thin. She was flat-chested. She had little self-confidence. But when she transferred to a different college, frosted her hair before arriving, and accumulated more modish outfits than many of the other female students, she suddenly found herself dating frequently for the first time in her life.

Her confidence improved.

Through that fall she dated one guy regularly, but it became apparent that they weren't well matched. He eventually broke it off.

After Christmas break, another guy who had been watching her decided he wanted to ask her out. So he talked to Fall Boyfriend to see if there was anything still going on.

"Oh, no!" said Fall Boyfriend. "She's a great person, but I could never get serious with anyone that flat-chested."

New Guy watched as she talked with friends waiting to enter the dining room. She was wearing a Lanz-knit T-dress, the color of orange sherbet with dark brown trim. Her tights were orange sherbet and she had on t-strap brown shoes with square heels. She was laughing. He thought, "She's got guts. She isn't afraid to wear a form-fitting knit dress even though she's so skinny."

Several years later, New Guy and the girl got married. He told her the story behind why Fall Boyfriend stopped dating her. She went on the Pill. She gained a little weight. She sewed herself a groovy outfit with a knit turtleneck and a knit pinafore over-top. She felt confident.

They returned to their former college campus in the spring for a visit. In the music building elevator Fall Boyfriend stepped on as she was riding alone to the third floor. Her posture was straight. Her figure was

cute. He couldn't stop staring at her chest.
　　The doors opened and she exited the elevator.
　　She burst into laughter.
　　Best laugh.

Parents Are The Worst

The school bus lets me off at the bottom of the hill on Williamsburg Drive. Part of the way I walk with other kids from my street, and then the last little bit I am on my own, skipping down the hill and up the sidewalk to our front door. I knock. No answer.

Where could my mother be? She's always here when I get home from school. I try getting into the house through the cellar windows, which open within a half-circle of metal siding. Locked. Where is she? And then the fearful thought...could the Rapture have gobbled everybody up and I've been left because I didn't believe hard enough? Panic. Is it minutes or an hour before she drives up? By the time she parks the car, I nearly faint from the anxiety. When you've heard all of your eight or nine years that the Lord will come back and whisk away only those who are really saved, and you are always feeling that maybe you haven't gotten this believing thing right, this is horrible to contemplate. And when you return to an empty house that usually has a welcoming parent there, but now you are alone outside—welcome to the world of a sensitive, frightened child raised in Pre-Millennial Rapture Eschatology.

Parents sometimes act under noble intentions but end up causing pain or resentment. I'm sure that my own children have experienced something similar with me.

I know now as an adult that my parents thought they were guiding us kids down a sound path.

Whew. Parenting is a bitch.

Trash On The Ground

Sometimes the school bus let us out at the end of Haymaker Road and we'd walk the long way home. One day there was a candy bar, still in its wrapper, just sitting there along the road in the grass. Since we were rarely allowed to eat any candy at all, I considered this hitting the ultimate jackpot. It was one of those candy bars with five little squares on a flat surface, each filled with a different flavor—peanut butter. caramel, nougat and such.

   I quickly dismantled and proceeded to devour the treasure. I think I already knew that I shouldn't litter, so I brought the wrapper home with me. Smokey the Bear was smiling down at me with glistening white teeth. That good girl…picking up litter.

   By taking the wrapper home in my book bag, my crime of not only eating a whole candy bar but eating a whole candy bar that might have been laced with poison by a disgruntled chocolate factory worker was discovered.

   This must have happened before the time I found a pack of Camels with one cigarette in it on the other end of Haymaker Road. That "find" culminated in being discovered by my mum since I kept it to play grownup games with friends like Secretary, or Telephone Operator. Grownups back then smoked in all kinds of jobs and public places. So, of course, it was a prime prop for make-believe.

   On that occasion my mum shamed me by saying, "What would Pastor Garman think?" Or, "What would Jesus think of you with cigarettes?" I was eight years old.

   Somehow I survived both the possibly-poisoned candy and "smoking" an unlit cig.

I still look for treasures abandoned or tossed along the road. My mum would be so disappointed.

Childhood Fears

First grade in an eight room, red-brick schoolhouse in Monroeville, PA. That old building is now gone, replaced by a sad attempt of modernity with a glass and metal office building. In 1954, it housed four first grades on the first floor, four second grades on the upper floor, a basement that contained restrooms for children, and a cafeteria that always smelled like old cheese (I wonder where the teachers went to the bathroom?). The floors were tiled with large squares of two-toned linoleum...well, I think they were large. Everything seemed large back then. The stairs to the basement were big and dark. The school bus that took me to this school was large, the older kids were large, Miss Martin was definitely large in my eyes.

My brother had contracted polio when I was four. I had watched his reflection in the mirror over the iron lung so many times and sat in his innumerable therapy and doctor appointments. I had a foreboding feeling about all things medical.

Spring of 1955 arrived, along with the Salk polio vaccine. All school children were to be vaccinated. This meant a bus ride from our small school on one of those large buses to an even larger junior high school across town. It entailed lining up in alphabetical order with absolutely NO talking or fidgeting as we waited. The aforementioned Miss Martin (who had slapped a ruler beside my hand earlier in the year when I peeked to see how to spell 'please' on a spelling test) was vigilant, stalking up and down the line of small children waiting to file out of our large classroom across the large floor tiles.

My last name of Witherspoon always placed me either last in line or close to last. I can still see my little self wearing my spring coat, anticipating the worst, quietly hopping back and forth on the tiles to keep my mind off the dreaded shot (another fear). I don't think I was talking, just sidling back and forth to distract myself.

Suddenly Miss Martin was looming over me and speaking loudly. "You are to stand still and be quiet!" I was mortified. I wasn't a kid who acted out, although my final report card said that I needed to learn to not talk so much. I froze and gulped. Like a lamb to the slaughter, I followed the line of other first graders onto the bus.

As I recall, the apprehension increased as we formed yet another line at the junior high. The nurse who administered the vaccine was kinder. I lived.

I lived, and I never contracted polio. So, scary as it was, it was worth it.

1+2=3

My mother used to say that having two close friends at the same time was tricky. Someone would inevitably feel left out.

In the 1950s my family lived in a suburb of Pittsburgh. My house was a newer one on Williamsburg Drive with a lot of brick tract homes. Just one lot away was an unpaved, gravel road that connected our street to the older, more established Haymaker Road. This connecting road ran through some undeveloped land and was embraced by large trees whose branches held hands overhead, so walking to Carol's house felt like a walk in the country. Continuing to Haymaker, things were more established—older homes built of stone with groomed yards and shrubs trimmed into shapes intermingled with some more modern brick houses. This is where the morning school bus stop was, right in front of Susie's house.

We three girls rode the same bus to school every day for a couple years. I would leave my house, walk up the gravel road, stop at Carol's house, and we would meet Susie at the bus stop. There was a continual power shift in the threesome. Who would sit with whom on the bus? Where would we play after school?

Some days we'd all play together at Carol's. She lived in a rock house on a remnant of a farm property that still had chicken coops and beehives. Her dad let us fix up an abandoned henhouse as a playhouse. It was tall enough to stand in and had real windows in it. All sorts of fruits hung on the trees scattered around the enormous backyard. Her next-door neighbor was her aunt who did things like canning. Carol had a younger brother, Ralphy, who was always butting in during our playtime.

Other days we'd play at Susie's in her "modern" yellow-brick tract home. She had an older brother who was a pest, but her mother always had the TV on, which wasn't happening at my house because we didn't even have a TV for most of my elementary school years. Susie was more of a bossy type, so if Carol and I wanted to play on our own we had to sneak around and not let on what we were doing.

I can't recall that these girls came to play at my house all that much. Maybe it was the fact that we had no TV. I do recall somehow getting hold of mercury out of a broken thermometer and sitting on my bedroom floor, rolling it into smaller pieces and then rejoining it in a big blob. These were also the friends who played "office" with me when I found the lone cigarette walking up the gravel road. Maybe after my mum discovered that, she curtailed playtimes at our house. Or since the school district constantly moved its borders, we may have ended up in different schools and on different buses. The friendships weren't lifelong, obviously, but germane to my childhood.

Whenever one of us felt on the outs with the other two, my mum would repeat her observation about three friends.

Throughout my life I've had other sets of two close friends. Maybe my mum's admonition has affected the way I look at that now. It basically means being an adult with two friends is not tricky, it's enriching. It means that sometimes the whole group functions brilliantly and sometimes one person may need to have personal time alone. It means that if two of us go to a movie without the other, we don't boast about it, but, if asked, we give a brief review. It means that all of us kvell when something good happens to one and empathize when one feels sorrow or pain.

I know I didn't always experience this; the tendency to fear being left out is a strong one. But it's a choice, isn't it, how I weigh the need to be included against the treasure of having two friends?

To Those Who Have Shown Me Love

The movie theatre is dark and very quiet except for sniffling. We are near the end of the documentary about Fred Rogers. One of the participants in the film suggests that we take a minute to remember someone who made us feel loved or showed us how to love others because that is a very "Rogerian" experience.

I dig for the wadded-up Kleenex in my purse and wipe my eyes for the fifth or sixth time. Then I remember, too.

My takeaway is that, despite the fact that I have felt unloved at times throughout my life, many kind faces still float into my memory-eye.

My dad who told me repeatedly when I was little what a beautiful baby I was (even though my mum had said I was a rather typically prune-like newborn).

A woman who was a younger friend of my mother who bolstered my adolescent insecurities by chatting with me when she plucked my unibrow.

My mum who loved me through the heartbreak of a broken engagement by letting me know that the guy didn't deserve me and someday I would see that. (I have; he turned out to be a Tea-Party-ish fundamentalist, rah-rah military pastor).

My parents who loved and held my little son when I was coping with the news of his severe disabilities. They surrendered pure, unconditional love to him, and to me who took a long time to "get my act together".

Two friends who mentored my husband and me were generous in helping us financially in rough times, built us up as we struggled with raising a son who had disabilities and a daughter who went through the usual teenage kerfuffles.

My husband whom I repeatedly had hurt by break-ups when we dated but who wrote me in 1971, "I have always loved you and I hope you will visit me in Colorado." I did. Four months later we were married. Forty-six-and-a-half years later we still are, and he can still quietly show me that I am loved.

Best Birthday Present EVER

In 2002, I got the most unique and "best" present ever.

My daughter was expecting her first child and her due date was June 25. Because she and her husband had asked me to stay (for a month!), we had arrived in Flagstaff the weekend before, to celebrate my birthday early and their second wedding anniversary, also on June 25. My daughter is a planner, an organizer, a magician on schedules, so with our calendar up-to-date, at her suggestion, we decided to go out for dinner on the twenty-fourth. That would make it only a day to the due date.

We ordered, and suddenly my daughter had this faraway look in her eyes. I didn't even notice it until my husband pointed out that it was the same expression I had years before, when I was entering the first stages of labor. A sort of "I'm not really here with the rest of you" look. Before even finishing their dinner, my daughter and son-in-law got up and drove home to wait things out.

My husband and I went to our Bed and Breakfast and somehow fell asleep. At three in the morning, the phone rang and my daughter's voice breathlessly said, "Hi, Nana."

Gemma had arrived exactly on her due date! It was a day early for my birthday, but undoubtedly the most exciting present to experience. Within hours of her arrival we all learned that she was born with a soft cleft palate and that turned the joy into apprehension and sadness, given that my husband and I had parented a child with special needs ourselves, and we knew there might be some hard times ahead.

I didn't stay a month (my suggestion), but I was there those first two weeks as my daughter and son-in-law navigated the mystery of a newborn who might or might not be dealing with some serious issues. In nine days that 'birthday baby' will be sixteen. Surgery has repaired what was damaged. She is a confident, talented, bright, and funny young woman.

I'm going to share this with her. For my birthday this year.

Catching Up With Poppop

You know—when I was small you were my favorite grandparent. You were funny and gentle and patient, and you made great pancakes for breakfast when we kids stayed overnight.

Where did you get the sense of mischief and fun? Were either of your parents like that? I only vaguely recall your father who frightened me—I guess because he was old and I was still very young. Were you at all close to him?

Your mom—I know she was the one who instilled a love for literature and writing in you and your siblings. I wish I could have met her. I wish I could hear stories about her and how she came from Liverpool to Western Pennsylvania.

How did you end up fighting in the first World War? You always seemed to be such a man of reasonable peace, a guy who avoided conflict. Was it the times? Were all Americans caught up in fighting back then? I know that you were one of the last to reach France and now when I read over your journal, I see what a pure, thoughtful man you were even in that horrifying place.

When you repaired the machine gun under fire, I wonder what you were thinking. You were a new husband; you obviously were very in love with Alma, or Peg as you called her. I wish so much I could talk to you and see what went through your mind. Were you in the trenches?

Then I think about the time when I knew you as a teen and adult—when I was a young mother with my own children. It always baffled me that you were so long-suffering when Nana berated and mistreated you. Now it's rare to see someone have that kind of patience. Was it your own upbringing? Your faith? Your love for her? Was she different when you

fell in love with her and married her before shipping out to France?
I see you in the backyard on Caruso Drive—spraying the rose bushes (was that kerosene?) or trimming the grape arbor. I see the day I watched Queen Elizabeth's coronation at your house on the TV and how you made me a crown out of a paper bag. You were artistic and creative. I get tears thinking about how much you must have hurt when my family moved so far from Pennsylvania to Memphis…your only daughter, your only grandchildren.

Good Neighbor

I awoke to my phone buzzing at me. It was my daughter, which was unusual—we don't do a lot of phoning with each other, but I was pleased that she had called. As we chatted, something she said drifted across my mind's eye....a date....and then I got this sick feeling in my stomach because while I was trying to talk to her, my brain was also trying to glom onto something that I'd forgotten. I finally excused myself from the call and rushed to the computer calendar and there was the proof—I had completely forgotten an MRI appointment scheduled for earlier that morning.

Which brings me to another thought—sometimes a good neighbor is the person who shows up when we don't even know we need help.

Recently, during a trip to New York, I was experiencing what I now know was pain from arthritis in a hip. I was making my way from Roosevelt Island to Manhattan with my wheeled suitcase and a backpack purse. I did some snappy descending of the escalators in the Roosevelt Island subway station, but when I got to the last level there were concrete stairs. Deep breath. I started cautiously down a step when out of nowhere, a young man came alongside and offered to carry my case the rest of the way down.

And then, leaving the subway on the Manhattan side, another flight of stairs loomed before me. Down the stairs came a cheerful young man who stopped as I clumped up step by pain-filled step and insisted he take my bag back up to the street. Two good neighbors who were total strangers within ten minutes of each other.

I think that is what the parable of the Good Samaritan is about—people of different backgrounds and origins helping a stranger.

So Many Pets To Feed

When our son Gavin first moved out with supported living, one of his first goals was to have a pet of his own. He had always loved our goofy black cocker spaniel. He also enjoyed being around the cats that we'd had.

So, he and his roommate, an "able-bodied" young man, went to the shelter and brought home two of the most gorgeous cats ever. One was pure white fluff which they named "Q-tip", and the other was an orange and white mix, "Tigger". Unfortunately, several months later Q-tip was either hit or poisoned and found by one of the assistants in the driveway of the back house where Gavin was living. Tigger remained as an outdoor cat, since the roommate's idea of caring for a feline was to stick its litter box in Gavin's closet and forget to clean it until there was a Himalayan mountain range in it (This was the same roommate that left Gavin on the toilet one night at 10 pm, fell asleep, and never took him off the toilet until the morning assistant arrived. Not what we'd call a person who paid attention to detail.).

One cat tragically gone, one roommate immediately gone. Gavin's next roommate was a peach of a young man who was allergic to cats, so Tigger still remained outside. When the time came for Gavin to move to a bigger apartment, Tigger came to live with my husband and me because landlord's rules included no pets. Since he was already used to being outdoors, we acclimated him by having him live in the garage and gradually letting him out with supervision. He was a charming guy, not particularly the cuddly type, but he caught rats and showed up on time for his kibble at our back door.

One night I went to the backdoor to check his bowl, since he sometimes took vacations from us, and to turn off the porch light. To my amazement, he was sitting patiently, staring at the door, and next to him was a baby possum. They were sitting like dogs do when waiting for a reward of a treat. After a squeal of surprise (from me, not them), I put some kibble out and they both ate from the bowl.

This went on for some time—a few weeks—and the baby possum turned into an adolescent and then a young adult. What astounded me was that they were "pals". Possums can be vicious, and cats are also known for their hunting, but there they were, cozying up to the buffet for all they could eat.

When we sold the house, the new owners said they wanted Tigger to stay. He roamed that neighborhood for several years, eating at one house, sleeping in the garage of another, and earning his keep by catching mice. As far as I know, he did this solo—his possum sidekick had moved on.

Meddlesome People

Probably one of the most uncomfortable combos of character is that of the People-pleaser and the Meddler. The Meddler will insert herself (in my experience the Meddler is usually of the female gender), while the People-pleaser will kowtow while seething or go to great lengths to make an excuse instead of saying with a smile, "Not talking about that, not going."

For years I have been the People-pleaser. There may be others who have me categorized as a Meddler, but no one except my kids has openly confronted me with that description.

I have gone along with the Meddler's intrusions into my income, my housing status, my marital relationship, my children's lives, my holiday plans, my church attendance (or lack thereof), my avoidance of dreaded ladies' luncheons, my absence from Tupperware or Cookie Lee Jewelry parties.

Only a few years ago did I learn (from my daughter, of all people) that I did not have to remain a People-pleaser. I could actually say "No thank you" and leave it at that. I did not have to invent a clever but truthful excuse. I did not have to go to events or serve on another committee if I didn't want to. I could be "authentic" while being polite and take nothing personally if the Meddler was put off by the New Me. (Credits to The Four Agreements.)

It's not an easy transition.

But it's pretty great.

Meddler: You really need to _____.

Me: No, I won't be _____.

Meddler: But why?

Me: I won't be _____.
(Repeat as needed).
Smile.

My Favorite Book

Gavin was born on an ice-slick night. He was about five weeks early but weighed just a bit more than a preemie. A week after his birth, he had still not opened his eyes. We began to worry, until one morning, as Larry held him by a window where the sun brilliantly reflected on the snow, his eyes opened... and our worry grew. It was at that moment when we realized something was terribly wrong.

Thus began a journey for us as a family that was oftentimes excruciatingly painful and full of apprehension for Gavin and for all of us.

Gavin didn't sleep through the night for nearly a year. Many days as soon as I could get him and his toddler sister down for naps, I would crash too. But some days I lay across the bed with "The Forsyte Saga"—a trilogy of novels by John Galsworthy that recounted several generations of well-to-do Brits and the intrigues of love and duplicity that spilled over, wrecking many in the family.

It was my escape. For a while I wasn't in Memphis with an infant who was a mystery to me or the wife of a struggling graduate school student working several part-time jobs to support us or the mum of a little two-year-old who I feared would also be negatively affected by our circumstances. I was in London and its environs in the early part of the twentieth century, following characters whose lives erased my own reality.

That book kind of saved my sanity.

Just a little detour here—in my elementary and junior high years, I read and re-read all the Betsy-Tacy and Tib books by Maud Hart Lovelace. It's kind of funny that both my adult and childhood favorites were set in the early 1900s.

A Song, A Memory

My first favorite song was "The Swan" from Carnival of the Animals by Camille Saint-Saens.

I was only four or five when my mother took me to the Carnegie Museum Music Hall in Pittsburgh to see the Salzburg Marionettes. They danced to this song at one point, and this moment remains with me today.

That night, in the bunk bed I shared with my younger brother, that music was still so present to me. I can close my eyes now and see the light under the bedroom door from the bathroom opposite the hallway, and remember how the music overwhelmed me with love for my mother because she had treated me to something so ethereal.

Passing Notes

The school I attended from sixth grade through my senior year was a Memphis attempt at grandeur. It housed all grades K-12, had enormous Supreme Court-like pillars over the grand entrance, marble floors in the main hall, and classrooms with high ceilings. On the backside of this impressive building was a long, bunker-style addition with skylights in the ceilings, because there were no other outside windows except for one room at the end occupied by Mrs. Miller, the formidable seventh-grade English teacher. She was my homeroom teacher and a stickler for diagramming sentences, crossing double "t"s in words separately, and keeping order.

A couple doors back in this Annex, as it was called, was the room of a neurotic teacher who taught spelling. I can't remember her name but I know that she was extremely eccentric and that students misbehaved in her class because she sat at her desk doodling fantastical stuff as we were ordered to maintain silence. Our classes were seated alphabetically, so I was always at the back of the room (since I was Witherspoon). On the same row but closer to the front was my close friend Carolyn Staten. Somewhere near her was another classmate, a sweet, bright but nerdy girl, Kathy Snodgrass.

One day, to alleviate the boredom of writing vocabulary words ten times each and putting them in sentences, Carolyn and I carried on a surreptitious note-passing activity. One of us—I THINK it was Carolyn—used the phrase "BoogerBushes" to write something mean-spirited about Kathy. Miss Neurotic Spelling Teacher intercepted it and proclaimed to the class that the two of us were writing obscenities!

Now, remember, I was always a good girl, afraid to break rules. This was enough to make me want to pass out. The teacher handed our note over to the principal, who then handed it to Mrs. Miller. Mrs. Miller phoned my mother and Carolyn's mother, and without giving details, called an emergency summit to discuss the fact that their daughters were part of an obscenity letter writing ring.

The mothers met that week with Mrs. Miller who produced the note with the "obscenity" of BoogerBushes. My mother reported later that she could barely refrain from guffawing but maintained decorum. It was decided that Carolyn and I would apologize sincerely to Kathy for using that nickname. I don't think we got any other punishment… maybe extra sentences to diagram.

As I write this, I reflect on how cruelty and bullying has always been a part of life for kids who have odd-sounding names, or look different from the popular students, or are smarter (or not as smart) than others. I am ashamed to think that my little Christian self would have been a "mean girl". Maybe that spelling teacher herself was an outcast in the faculty ranks, maybe she knew the pain of being the target of name-calling, maybe she just wanted to curtail something that could have grown out of control.

Thinking about my mum's reaction, I am so appreciative that she didn't blame me or punish me. She was not generally a snarky name-caller herself, but she did have a keen sense of humor and recognized that "BoogerBushes" was not an obscenity. Ironically, she and Kathy later became friends in a Bible study my mother held for teenagers.

Silence

Last week I had the beautiful experience of sitting on a trail in Sedona, Arizona, where the only sounds were insects chirping and birds scratching their way up the scrub oak branches. I was on a hike with my husband and friends; I got the sensation in my barometer hip that I needed to halt the climb. So I sat down with a book and read a little, but I mostly reveled in the silence.

At one point, a noisy helicopter ferrying tourists over the trail disrupted the peacefulness, but it was soon gone. Only one other hiker passed me.

It was a curative experience.

As I was mulling this over after returning home, I had a vivid memory of another time when silence was terrifying.

Freshman year of college for me was at a small Christian liberal arts college nestled in the Ozarks of Arkansas. The dorm I lived in was built in the 1920s. It was a three-story affair, with the college cafeteria taking up the basement floor and a long outdoor stairway leading up to the main common area of the girls' dorm. There were a few dorm rooms on that floor but most of them were on the top floor. My roommate and I shared a room facing out to the campus commons.

The college was located in a tiny town called Siloam Springs and was surrounded by farmland. At night there was little light and minimal noise (like basement machinery and the occasional clank of a water pipe). Our dorm rooms were not air-conditioned, so we often had the windows open.

The year I began college was the same year that Richard Speck murdered eight student nurses in Chicago. This was still on a lot of students' minds in the following spring.

One night, an odd sensation woke me. I could feel a total absence of noise, as though it were pressing down on my eardrums. No machinery, no crickets, no pipes. I woke my roommate because I had to go down the hall to the communal restroom. We were both frightened, our minds bloody with murdered nurses. What if a Richard Speck copycat had entered our dormitory? What if he was hiding somewhere on our floor? Christine grabbed a hand mirror with a long handle to use as a weapon if we needed it.

The restroom had long mirrors over the sinks that reflected the entire room, so while we were breathlessly trying to finish our business, one of us saw the reflection of the other in the mirror. This was the final straw. 'Someone' was in the restroom with us! We grabbed each other and our mirror weapon and without realizing what we were doing, we bolted down the hall screaming at the top of our lungs. We didn't want to be alone in our own room so we headed to the room of our most formidable friend, a girl named Shirley whose father had developed Sikorsky helicopters. In our frenzy, I guess we thought she could fight off an attacker better than the rest of us skinny little white girls.

Silence can be a golden treasure. It can also be the catalyst to terror.

Snowy White

They both had snowy white hair, my grandmothers, and they took great care and pride in that. I remember they would often pull their hair into a roll at the nape of the neck or wind it into tight curls on the sides. They seemed almost otherworldly to a little girl with her own thick head of non-descript light-brown hair. I would watch them as they stood at their dresser mirrors, placing hairpins just-so, picking up a hand-mirror to check the back. When my first grandmother died, she had shifted her hairstyle to a short, permed look, cute and elegant. But my other grandmother wasn't so lucky. She died after many years of being bedridden with Alzheimer's, her hair had grown long and unkempt. My grandfather had to pull it into a ponytail. She was like a reproduction of Miss Havisham from "Great Expectations", lying silent in her bed and staring uncomprehendingly at me. If she had been aware of how she looked, she would have been horrified.

My own mother's hair began to go gray and then white when she was in her 30s. For many years she did the weekly "hair appointment" with a guy she claimed was the only one who could back-comb three hairs to look like a full head of hair, since her hair was extraordinarily thin even then. The appointment included ash-blonde coloring and, later, after "fro" perms came out, she did that too. However, in her seventies she began to let her hair grow a little longer, and she stopped coloring it. I have one beloved snapshot of her and my dad enjoying an evening out in Stuart, Florida, and her hair is curly and chin-length. As she succumbed to Alzheimer's much like her mother did, it became easier and less traumatic for her to just leave her hair uncut and pulled back with barrettes or a hair band. She too developed that facial expression of bewilderment at who she was and where she was.

Often, as I pass a mirror or walk into the bathroom without my glasses on, I catch a glimpse of myself, a woman who is seventy and has longer white hair. They are all there—those two grandmothers and my mum. My grandson says I look like my paternal grandmother who didn't have Alzheimer's. I think I favor my own mum and her mother. It's not scary; it's rather like having a vision of the future that one can't do anything to alter.

It is what it is.

Optimism

One birthday, my parents gave me a card with a funny little man in a yellow slicker and hat, holding an umbrella with a dejected expression on his face. Above him the sun was shining brightly and a little duck was gawking at him in consternation. The message was "Happy Birthday to a confirmed Pessimist." I've kept it for fifty years meaning to frame it.

You see where I'm going with this, right?

Optimism is not my gift.

I figure that it's safer not to be optimistic and then be disappointed. That way, when things crash, you're prepared. There's no huge disappointment. Just a sense of satisfaction. "I knew that all along."

OK.

I'll close with something more upbeat. I just saw RBG, the marvelous documentary about our dear Ruth on SCOTUS. Watching how she went to law school as a new young mother, got on Harvard Law Review, and won six out of seven cases she argued before the Supremes, culminating in her appointment in the '90s by Clinton—that made me optimistic. Heaven knows that we will need dozens of clones of her to break through the putrid barricade we are facing presently. If a young woman raised in Brooklyn in the '30s and '40s by an immigrant father and a strong second-generation mother can rise to this height and fight the good fight for the under-represented, I have to have some optimism that it can happen again.

In my lifetime—please!

How To Dress Properly And Influence People

It's the 1960s in Memphis, Tennessee. If you live in East Memphis, and if you are female, you wear basically the same clothes as all the other East Memphis girls.

You have a wardrobe of A-line skirts and round-collared oxford cloth blouses and enough bar pins or circle pins to change your jewelry up regularly. The skirts in winter have coordinated cardigan sweaters. In warm weather, the blouses are short-sleeved or even sleeveless, but in winter, they have long sleeves and most of the time these blouses are white.

Your ensemble also includes headbands that are color-coordinated with the outfits. They may be plastic but very frequently they are fabric and can include your embroidered monogram (just in case you want to venture out and be a tiny bit independent). You don't have pierced ears (yet) but you wear rings on your hands, often your high school ring which is overpriced and for which you must save up a hefty amount of money in order to purchase in your junior year of high school.

Regarding footwear—this would usually be a loafer of some sort or flats. Sandals are not usually worn except on very informal occasions. Stockings are worn to school held in place by long-line girdles which you wear even if you weigh only ninety-five pounds because... well, just because (panty hose are only recently coming into vogue). You may also wear tights in colder weather with A-line jumpers that will have a round-collared blouse or a mock-turtle neck top underneath.

No need to fear—you look exactly like all the other girls who are in your group or in the group that you wish you belonged to.

Pulling Down Fences

Chopin Nocturne plays in the background.

The afternoon sky grows glum in preparation for the day's rain.

Morose, she sits and mulls over the meaning of the old adage, "You shall love your neighbor as you love yourself." She asks herself, "What if everyone did that?"

She has heard this Bible verse again and again since childhood, and it has always puzzled her because she so often has not loved herself. The times when she began to find things self-lovable, she'd quickly rein in that notion because...... she was also steeped in the notion that, like everyone in the world, she was born a sinner and had gone astray (even at age five or so).

As time passed, there were moments when she began to see herself through the eyes of her neighbors—not literally the people next door—but the people she encountered in life. Weren't they all her neighbors? And those neighbors gave her a sensation of being valued, of mattering in their lives, of seeing qualities in her that they thought were fun and endearing. Gradually, she left behind (as well as she could) the perception that she couldn't be loved. Of course she could. If those neighbors and the One she believed undergirded all Life and Creation really loved her, she could try to transfer that to the neighbors and the One, couldn't she?

She had to start backwards. The love came to her. Then she could give it back.

Free Ice Cream

"Some."

That's what I called ice cream when I first learned to speak. My parents would ask, "Want some?" and I logically deduced that was what you called the yummy, cold, sweet stuff.

I didn't have to worry for many years about paying for ice cream. There was always a parent or grandparent nearby who picked up the tab.

One grandmother got hand-packed ice cream (always vanilla) at the Rexall drugstore. The soda jerk would put a paper box inside a metal box and drop scoops of ice cream inside until the ice cream was jam-packed. Then he'd close the carton up like a box. Voila. A pint of ice cream to take home for dessert.

This same grandmother insisted that one NEVER licked an ice cream cone if one were a lady. Seriously, I can remember standing at an ice cream stand that sold soft frozen custard and getting a cone as a treat but having to take bites out of it! My grandfather would pick up the tab on those treats.

Around this time, Pittsburgh was dotted with a chain of delis called Isaly's. Checkered floors, soda fountain, and a little ice cream shop were at each location. We'd order chipped ham sandwiches and Owl potato chips. For dessert we'd usually get an ice cream cone that featured a tall, dare I say, almost phallic-shaped scoop of ice cream. I wouldn't have known that adjective to describe the cone then, by the way. I always got chocolate chip. Dad or Mum paid for those.

When we vacationed to Ft. Walton Beach in the Florida panhandle, the big final splurge of the week was lobster dinner in Destin and then a drive back to the Dairy Queen. Those cones were always the fudge-dipped ones. We'd finish them off quickly because of the dripping humidity and attack mosquitoes which punished us if we stood around too long. Daddy paid for those, too.

Throughout my marriage, we like to reward ourselves after being forced to perform onerous adult tasks, like doing taxes or heavy housecleaning. Often that means getting ice cream. When we first moved to California, we could treat our family of four for under a dollar, because Thrifty Drugstores sold cones for fifteen cents. Until Larry had to start watching his sugar intake, we would regularly take a walk in our quaint Southern California town and justify a dipped cone at DQ again— I don't think it can be classified as real ice cream, but life is short. Most of the time, Larry paid.

I don't think I have ever figured out what I'd do if I ordered a cone and didn't have money. Obviously, my pattern is to make sure I'm with someone who has cash.

Two Parties On The Same Weekend

It is a windy, crystal-laden Chicago winter in the late '60s, the kind that whips your long hair around as you walk briskly beside your newest heartthrob. You are headed to Kungsholm Restaurant with three or four other couples, to engage in a splurge of great proportions. Everyone is dressed to perfection. You are wearing a pale pink A-line wool dress with matching pink leather shoes.

The US and Swedish flags fly over the entrance, just under a model Viking ship. Inside, the surroundings are elegant, with Scandinavian décor in private dining rooms, white starched tablecloths with beautiful flatware and dishes, candles, flowers in bud vases. The waiters are impeccably polite and treat the gauche college kids with dignity. There is a bountiful Scandinavian smorgasbord laid out with artistry, not the kind at "all-you-can-eat" places. During the course of the dinner, a fishbone lodges in your throat. The attentive waiter rushes to the table suggesting how to best handle this embarrassing situation. Crackers, drinks of water (no alcohol, mind you) and much un-ladylike coughing ensues. The crisis passes, but attention has been drawn to you.

After the magnificent dessert, the group moves to the miniature theatre, which features marionettes performing a complete musical, Kismet. It's so romantic—the tiny dancers, the emotional songs, the glow of being with a boy who has suddenly swept you off your feet, even though you have been regularly dating another college man who is steady, kind, and generous. You wrap up in a heavy maxi coat and gloves, take the arm of your date, and venture into the even colder Chicago night to walk back along Rush Street to campus. You feel blissful.

But you have a bit of a problem because the next night, Sunday, the

Wonderful, Caring College Man has already planned a special date to surprise you. You try your best to relax and be sociable. Once again, you don the heavy coat and, once again, you walk through frigid temperatures to the mystery destination. With each block that you pass, your heart jumps a bit higher because you are going exactly the same direction as you did on Saturday night with the new Romeo. With a huge grin, Wonderful College Man stops at Kungsholm and says, "Surprise!" (This may be one of the first times you ever improvised being surprised and acting like you'd never been here.) Up the stairs you climb to the same dining room and, yes, there is the same waiter who rescued you from the fishbone. He is discreet. You still feel like a louse.

Once more you sit through Kismet, listening to "Stranger in Paradise" and wishing you could be somewhere else because you feel so duplicitous. Wonderful College Man doesn't suspect a thing. He is so thrilled to have planned this special evening for the two of you. Fickle, fickle woman.

Only some years later when Wonderful College Man proposes to you, and the two of you are married within four months, do you ever tell the story. He laughs.

That's because he really is Wonderful.

If The Shoe, Or Ring, Or Soda Can Tab Doesn't Fit

In the spring of 1965, I had fallen in love with a man who was a little older than I. He was from Harlingen, Texas, but had been stationed at the Navy-Marine base outside Memphis and came to the church that my family attended. He was very spiritual, said he wanted to be a missionary when he was discharged from the Marines. Even though he was not as cool as the guys I knew in Memphis, I was in thrall. He shipped out to Vietnam that autumn.

I don't remember a proposal per say, but somewhere in that freshman year he asked me to marry him. It might have been in a letter or he might have asked when he came to see me at college before he left. He asked me what kind of engagement ring I wanted, so I described a simple gold band with a Tiffany setting solitaire. I probably even sent a picture torn from a magazine. I expected that when he returned from Vietnam he'd present this to me in some romantic setting.

Sophomore year started. One afternoon I picked up my mail at the college post office and there was a small package from Jerry. I walked behind the women's dorm and sat on the steps overlooking the valley below as I opened the box. There was a diamond ring….a solitaire….in a setting that I can only describe as similar to the pull-top on a soda can. There was no note or anything. It fit perfectly. Awkwardly, I put the ring on my finger and went to my dorm room.

My two roommates squealed and jumped (as was the requisite), but I could tell they thought it was a bit weird. In fact, anyone who saw the ring had this rather awkward reaction. "Oh, is he back from 'Nam?"

When I went home for Christmas, my family was happy, but my mum knew me well enough that she saw my disappointment, not just in the actual ring, but in the way it had come to me.

In January of 1968, I returned home to plan a wedding and go to Memphis State. A week into the semester, Jerry shipped back from Vietnam. I flew to Harlingen to see him after a sixteen-month absence and to stay with his family that I'd never met. He took me to his church and everyone wanted to see the ring. His mother introduced me as "Jerry's little friend." He was not the same person that I had known before. There was a stilted, almost feigned warmth on his part. On the last night at his parents' home we sat up to talk, and he told me that he had had an affair in Kuala Lumpur on R&R, that I wasn't as sexy as he'd expected (he even asked if I wore a padded bra), and that he felt unworthy of me. He didn't actually break it off, he just left me hanging as he drove me the long, long, painfully long trip back to Memphis.

I should have thrown the damn pull-top ring at him right then and there, but I was in shock. I'd waited for so long, hadn't dated at all in his absence, and even though I knew in my heart it was better to find out all this before going through with a wedding, I was crushed. The afternoon after we got to Memphis, I took a long walk alone. My mother was returning from her job and saw me on the street and pulled over. I told her the whole story. She was so wonderful and enveloped me in a hug. She reminded me that there had always been little things that didn't seem to fit right, and that eventually this break-up could be a relief. That night I told him I wanted to end the engagement. I'm sure he was relieved.

A day or two later, Jerry drove off. Yes, he actually had the chutzpah to hang around after this. Before he left, I gave him the ill-fated soda can jewelry, although later I wished I had kept it and had the diamond made into an earring or necklace.

The idea of the engagement ring fit the dreams of Young College Girl who hadn't had any experience in romance. The ring was a terrible fit actually, but returning it also liberated me from a life tied to someone who would have been an awful match. He went on to be a missionary and eventually a conservative pastor who boasted about his guns and his fence installed with warnings on his property in Indiana. He probably knows Mike Pence. Talk about a bad fit.

Bonnie Is A Fine Girl

To Emalina, Paisley, and Sophie

Back when I was in my sixties and life seemed full of possibilities, I signed up for an improv class, dragging Amado, my husband, with me. He has a PhD in electrical engineering/physics, but as I'm always trying to fix him, to mould him into the liberal arts person that I could relate to. I was in my usual "what am I doing here" mode, "I'm the oldest one who am I trying to kid," etc. I did one improv where I was sitting on a park bench trying to convert Deb, who had white hair and was immaculately groomed in perfect taste and much freer than I was, into Christianity. It turned out that I was using the same techniques that she used to use when she identified as an evangelical. I was so pleased to have aced it. I had something to talk about with someone in class. Deb seemed to socialize with everyone, though, which annoyed me. I wanted her to myself. Soon Amado stopped going and returned to science and I went alone. I met Edna, who was adorable, and she and Deb seemed fearless in a sea of twenty-something pilgrims who had come to L.A. to make it in show business. There were other ages, too, but I managed to stay sulky and insecure. I'd skulk on the sidelines waiting for a pause in the action or an invitation to act. My lesson came from Lisa Fredrickson, an angel of a teacher who told me to barge in and interrupt. A life lesson for a boomer girl.

Deb moved to Flagstaff and I moved to New York City, but the move seemed to make our friendship grow. I got the idea to write for ten minutes a day and found a list of Canadian elementary school prompts, and in true improv fashion, Deb and Edna said, "Yes, and..." as did Peter, our editor, who I also met in an improv workshop, but in Austin. I feel so grateful to have found these people at this point in my life, although it would have been equally nice to have them show up earlier. They are true friends, and we "get" each other.

Edna wrote a piece about worrying about her permanent file when she was in school, and when she finally got to see it (spoiler alert) it said, "Edna is a charming girl". Deb was always a good girl. She still is. She is the most politically active person I know on Facebook, always looking to do the right thing. So I started digging into my paper mess and found a fifth-grade report card that had mostly B's and said, "Bonnie is a fine girl". That can be read so many ways, depending on where you put the accent. I still have some issues with Mrs. Weaver, but I can leave those for another day.

Adventures On Mono Lake

When I was living in California, I used to see bumper stickers that said, "Save Mono Lake" and I always thought, "Why? Fuck Mono Lake." Mono Lake was a nightmare.

I was twenty-two and went camping with my husband, Tim, and a couple of neighbors. The neighbor had a Jeep, and we piled all our primitive gear in the back and took off to camp on Mono Lake, before we hit the Sierras.

Our destination was an island in the middle of the lake. We piled our gear in an inflatable army-issue raft and took off for the island, paddling as we went, until the raft sprang a leak. We pulled ashore on a sandbar, crisscrossed the oars over the edges of the raft and piled our gear on top of the platform, got in the water, and swam to the island, pushing what was now a huge, top-heavy inner tube with attachments as we went. What we didn't know, because the water was cloudy, was that it was full of stalagmites, hidden in the brine, razor-sharp with the intention of slicing us.

I remember also that it was a dead lake, that there was no life except for some microscopic shrimp, but I could be wrong. It just added to the creepiness.

When we got to the island, the sun was beginning to set and it had started to drizzle. We pitched our tent across oars and found boards, and if we turned a little in our damp sleeping bags the entire tent would pitch.

The next morning we found the entire island swarming with seagulls, dead and alive, and the ground had muck that sucked at your feet and added to the misery. Walt. That was the name of our neighbor. Walt built a fire. I have a photograph of this, so we must have eaten something before the swim back, pushing the stupid raft and our mucky, damp possessions, and skinning what was left of our shins and feet.

Mono Lake is still there, according to Wikipedia, and it looks really pretty, but deadly.

Adultery

After Man has totally destroyed this planet, it's only natural for him to find something else to destroy. In Seymour, by J. D. Salinger, Seymour sees a little girl playing in the sun. There's a kitten, and a shaft of light on her golden hair, so Seymour, overcome with emotion throws a rock at her.

That is Man's nature. Horror films, detective films, disaster films all have a passion for destroying the virgin, the slut, the lovely young thing, as long as she's beautiful.

We stick pins in butterflies and impale them on the wall. We hunt and kill animals in the wild for trophies. We domesticate other animals to kill them for food or fur, sometimes just for the pleasure of killing them.

We pollute the rivers and oceans. New Yorkers are shocked when I tell them that plastic bags are outlawed in Los Angeles and Austin. "How do they get rid of their trash?" they ask (I told two friends and they both asked the same question).

I heard that the original meaning of "Thou shalt not commit adultery" was that one shouldn't mess with anything that was pure, sacred; a lake, a forest, a contract.

And I heard that pornography was exploiting that which should be pure; the opposite of art, which is illuminating that which is sublime or divine; or pointing to what other people might not recognize as sublime or divine.

So we are adulterers and pornographers, and when we've sucked the world dry we'll find a Virgin in the sky who can give birth to a new civilization.

Be Quiet

An environmentalist was talking on TV about noise pollution. His quest was to create a cubic foot of silent space in the Olympia forest where there would be no sound of human machines. No jets overhead, no traffic, nothing. I was really pissed off at people as usual, and usually the people in charge, whoever they are, or were at the time.

Why should that be so fucking hard? To have one small spot where you can go and only hear nature.

I got an ear infection in Puerto Rico in May. I had a small dry cough for a couple of days and as soon as we got off the ferry in Vieques, this raw pain started in my left ear. I knew I couldn't make it through the night, and because it was Sunday evening, and all medical emergencies happen on a Sunday evening, there were no pharmacies open and no doctors available.

Amado and I trekked to the market in the tropical heat, because there might be something there to ease the pain. I saw several ambulances on the way, and some people sitting around near them. I asked Amado to ask them about help because I don't speak Puerto Rican, only Mexican. Amado said that they were going to drive me to help because I'd have to pay for the ambulance.

The man drove us in his dusty Fairlaine up into the hills where there was a tent. He knocked on the flap and nothing happened. I was so afraid of the pain by now that I was losing it, but I don't think anyone noticed. I have a very quiet way of catastrophising.

After a few minutes, a middle-aged woman opened the tent. She looked surprised to see us, and not thrilled. But we walked in anyway. I don't remember any invitation. There were several women sitting around a table inside.

They looked up startled, frowning. Amado explained what was happening and they asked for my insurance cards. I silently thanked myself for having them with me, and actually found them in the upper side pocket of my black crossbody Baggallini. One woman held out her hand for them and wrote down the information. They told me that another one of them was a doctor.

One woman took my blood pressure. Another took me into the corner and had me drop my pants and gave me a shot that had me sitting on my left cheek for three days. They told me I had an eye infection too, and found eye drops in a collection of little bottles another woman had brought to the doctor.

The doctor wrote a prescription for antibiotics, and one of the women drove us down into town to our bed and breakfast.

When the plane finally landed in New York, the pain was almost unbearable. It was unbearable but the plane landed anyway. I went to my allergist who gave me more antibiotics.

I then fell down on Third Avenue and went to see an ENT because I still couldn't hear out of my ear. The ENT gave me more antibiotics and Prednisone. After two move visits I can hear again, but there's a crackling noise when I swallow, and tinnitus, like someone is rubbing aluminum foil on a Formica kitchen counter. I stopped going to all the doctors, because I've had enough. I read that there's nothing they can do about tinnitus, anyway, that I will always have aluminum foil, no matter where I go, or what I do. When I walk it kind of jingles, like a burnt-out lightbulb.

I guess what I'm saying is that the square inch of silence that the environmentalists are fighting for would be wasted on me. I bless the metallic sputter of the air conditioner, the sound of jet skis going by in the East River, the distant sound of traffic on FDR Drive, and, of course, the iPhone.

Broken Leg

There was a teachers' strike in 1989, and I was on the union steering committee at Lincoln High School. I loved it! I loved that we stopped complaining and took action. This was what I was born to do. My dad had been a union organizer in the teachers' union in New York, and I was so ready. Starting salary for a teacher was $23,000 and there was an advertisement for electricians in the L.A. Unified Bulletin starting at $52,000. There were fifty-plus administrators making over $200,000. We were ready.

The first day of the strike Rosie, my eight-year-old, got knocked down on the playground. There obviously wasn't enough supervision, what with the strike and all, so I took her to Lincoln with me. I had to run across the street to talk to some people and told Rosie to wait at the corner. I sprinted across the street, heard a screeching of brakes and an impact, and turned around and Rosie was lying in a pool of blood in the middle of Lincoln Boulevard.

A crowd had gathered. I ran to her and sat next to her until the ambulance came. I can't say what I was feeling. I can't describe it or be there.

The ambulance took her to County General, the closest hospital to Lincoln. I had to leave the room several times to gain my composure and come back. At one point they wheeled in a woman who had committed hara kiri on herself, on one side of Rosie; on the other, a two-year-old who had been mauled by a pit bull.

I called my ex, who yelled at me.

I called my minister, who told me that all was well. That all would be fine, that I knew that, that I was divinely guided, and that I knew what to do.

They wanted to send her to an orthopedic hospital and I said no. Children's Hospital. I remember wheeling her up the stairs, and clouds ,and cute children's decorations. They put her in traction and she stayed in the hospital for two or three weeks. I remember the room was filled with balloons, many attached to stuffed animals. The balloons became almost sinister, obstructing nurses and doctors.

The school librarian came to visit and told the story of what it was like to see us there in the middle of the street. I went to the bathroom and threw up. I stayed with Rosie in that room. After the three weeks they put her in a full body cast with her legs separated, an iron bar holding them apart, and a hole for her to pee out of. They gave us a wheelchair that reclined.

I had to teach summer school that summer, and the school was caddy corner from the house.

I remember leaving Rosie with my twelve-year-old a few times. I think I got robbed by a babysitter, and after a few bad experiences I stopped trusting people. I remember seeing Hannah with Rosie in the wheelchair, and our golden retriever on the street.

I don't know how we made it through the summer, but I decided we had to get out of there. I quit teaching, took the top off the car, put Rosie in the cast, with the wheelchair in the car. A neighborhood boy helped me. I took off house hunting. I was obsessed with getting out of the neighborhood. Every spare minute I had I spent trying to buy a house near the church where I had support, where they kept saying that all was well, to turn it over to a higher power, that I was perfect, whole and complete.

From Up High

I spend a lot of time looking out at the New York City skyline and down below at the street from the eighteenth floor. People look not quite like ants, but like some sort of bug, and the jet skis, the cars, the bicycles are small toys that I don't relate to. If I were huge, I could squish them and not give it a second thought, the way I used to walk on ants as a little kid.

I'm sophisticated now. I have a couple of college degrees, but still, I engage in the fantasy.

Then what if ants have families, and by killing one you create a pain body that goes on for generations? What if the ant's significant others are forever traumatized? Just because they're small and we don't understand what it feels like to be an ant, doesn't mean that there isn't a whole universe going on inside an ant.

What about all those cars on FDR Drive? They're moving very slowly, but I don't care. They all have places to go and dinner to eat (too much of) and lives and universes that they place themselves at the center of. Or maybe they're just beetles.

Three sailboats are going down the river. There are no people sailing them, just microscopic dots at the bow. I have no sympathy for dots.

I don't care if those buildings fall or if a dot implodes. It's only later, when the newspaper publishes the articles, and the life stories, and the faces of the agony of those left behind that I care.

If one of those jet skis landed on my arm I'd flick it off. Someone on the jet ski has a sister like me, maybe. But it needs to be proven. People I don't know from above are an abstraction.

Closeness makes them real.

Window

Joseph Campbell said that in Buddhism, fear is one of the three temptations.

Until I was fifteen, we lived in a house on the side of a hill in Highland Park. The house, my mother said, was built by a cop in his spare time. I wanted to be where the action was. I didn't want to go to bed and miss what was happening upstairs in the living room, but I would be sent downstairs to bed, much too soon, alone, down the staircase.

About three-quarters down the stairwell was a high window—too high for me to see out of, about two-and-a-half or three feet in height, and maybe a foot-and-a-half or two wide. Outside I could only see the tops of tall avocado trees, the black night, and the unknown. I had the irrational terror that one night a hideous face would hover in that window, something that embodied evil, something more dangerous than anything I could imagine.

I didn't want to go to bed alone. They thought I was being manipulative, and they didn't want to put me to bed, and I felt like I was risking my life, and much more by doing so.

I had no fear of abandonment, actually I wished for it; no real fear of physical pain, of speaking, dancing, or singing in public, no fear of snakes or frogs or any animal, no fear of ocean waves, or roller coasters, but that window, the window into the darkness, chilled me like nothing else has since.

Walking Up The Walls And Across Ceilings

When I decided to move to Austin from Venice, California, I bought a house without seeing it in person. It was that fabulous. My budget was $250,000 and this was $249,000. It had four bedrooms and an office with a balcony, an open kitchen, French doors looking out at the Green Belt and central air. It was on a charming, winding street called Yellow Rose Trail. Yellow roses were my mother's favorite flower.

I moved in with $1,000 left to furnish it. I bought a king-sized mattress set for me, and a queen-sized set for the guest room. I was blissed out. All that wonderful space just for me, or so I thought. I took over the house two days before Christmas, but it wasn't until the early spring that I realized I wasn't alone.

It was a Monday in early April. I was standing in the bathroom and felt something on my arm. I looked down and there was a roach the size of a Buick resting gently on my forearm. I did what any non-Texan would do. I screamed my lungs out and danced around the house until I was spun around in the kitchen, gasping desperately like in a Hitchcock movie.

I never found out what happened to that exact roach, but later I was sitting on the floor (because I didn't have any furniture other than the beds) with my back propped against the bed, when I felt that same gentle tickle on my thigh. That was it. I went to sleep upstairs and called my first exterminator. They came highly recommended and were 100% organic.

I lived in that house seven years and had five different exterminating companies. I went from organic to environmentally toxic, kills everything and everyone, but nothing helped. The roaches would come in and die slowly, mostly. When they landed on the floor, I'd put a trash can over them, then if my son-in-law came he'd dispose of them for me. Amado would just stomp on them when he was visiting.

I'd watch their death throes, wondering if they felt pain, trying not to identify with them, feeling absolute horror. I remember one on the door jamb in the master bathroom. It was up there for hours, its arms and legs reaching towards me for help in a grotesque, sinister dance; the Dying Swan with six horrible legs and antennae.

Now, in New York, I found what looked like a ladybug on me. I didn't want to take it down in the elevator, but tried to put it in the hallway on a cardboard, but lost it on the way out.

I was tired. Being a Buddhist is exhausting.

Cooperation

Tom Johnson said, "God is a verb!" "If I move into action then God-as-me begins to exist."

There was a lot of talk in this religion, also, of the Christ within, the Christ being the creative part, the spark of the individual. So if creation is the act of the Christ, then lack of cooperation, or blocking the creativity is the antichrist.

You can see that in improv theatre, the antichrist. If someone says, "I'm going to open the window" and someone else says, "That's not a window it's a refrigerator," then the creation of the first person is wrecked.

I often accuse Amado of blocking our conversations; of arguing or countering my flights of fancy. His training was that of an engineer, and apparently that's what they do. It exhausts me.

You can see how Obama tried to do what he could to help people. Now Puff is trying to block, and undo, the creations of Obama.

I have this war going on within me now. I've got the push me-pull me going on with this keyboard: that which wants to create, and that which blocks it. That which wants to help people; that which says, "Leave me alone, I'm tired, I'm seventy-one for Christ's sake!"

Annette always quotes Jung. Apparently, what we don't embrace on the inside manifests on the outside in the collective consciousness.

When Obama was in the White House, the House and Senate's only purpose was to not cooperate with him. There could be no scene, no creation, no good.

One of my favorite improv games is when a group of five or six people get together to create a TV commercial, and everyone has to agree with and validate everyone else's ideas. You have five minutes to create this commercial. One person comes up with the concept; another, the product; another the marketing strategy; another the jingle. They perform the commercial in five minutes.

I would have the world be like this. My father always spoke about "Working together in the spirit of mutual cooperation" while we were doing dishes. He washed, my brother Bob and I would dry. Bob had a tendency to flip me in the butt with a damp towel. I had a tendency to get stomach cramps and run to the bathroom.

Thanksgiving

Mrs. Weaver was more than a teacher. She had a husband, and her husband painted the backdrops at the Museum of Natural History in Los Angeles. I went to see them and they looked very real. Their foreground was dead animals native to Southern California. They were stuffed and posed in different groupings to look alive. The room chilled me, even if I had a connection to the famous participant in the scenery. Do you have to kill something to admire it properly?

It was getting close to Thanksgiving and the third-grade classroom had orange and brown decorated bulletin boards and a display of dead corn and squash. We colored in mimeographed turkeys and made head bands with feathers and Pilgrim hats, and were given a homework assignment to write a poem about Thanksgiving. My dad was the editor of the poetry magazine at NYU when he was in college, and there was a lot of poetry around our house. I, myself, at eight, considered myself quite the poet, I guess, by osmosis, and went home to my cluttered room, sat at the second-hand children's desk, opened my notebook, and tackled it:

O I am thankful for the birds and the bees
And the beautiful rainbow that's over the trees....

Deep stuff. I brought my masterpiece to Mrs. Weaver the next day, and because I was the only one who wrote a poem, I guess, she read it to the class. She told the class that I wrote it, and I smiled with false modesty and soaked in the praise. She then did something that I thought was peculiar. She asked the class who should read the poem at the Thanksgiving assembly the following week? "What do you mean," I thought, "How can you even think of having someone else read it?" The class took a vote and it was decided that I should read it. "Wasn't that the obvious choice," I thought, but never said a word, because I didn't do that sort of thing. Mrs. Weaver then came up to my desk, handed me back the piece of paper with pathetic printing and said in a low voice that she thought I should change the phrase "that's over the trees" to "arches the trees".

"Sure," I said. I had no problem with that, but I felt a little uncomfortable. "Arches" seemed a little Longfellow to me, but I don't think I had the capacity to articulate that either.

The day of the assembly arrived, and I was called up to the microphone in front of the school assembly. Then Mrs. Weaver did something that would stay with me for the rest of my life. She announced to the assembly, "This is a poem that our class wrote, and please welcome Bonnie Arkin who will read it to us." I was so shocked I started to tremble, and couldn't distinguish between stage fright and the betrayal in my shaking.

What sticks to me this day is the fact that I didn't have a voice. I didn't have the capacity to say, "You know I was the one who wrote it! Why are you doing this? You made me add one stupid word, that I didn't even like, and now you're saying that the class wrote it? Does this make you look good somehow?"

I didn't say anything. If I have any regrets in life it would be that I lacked and still lack that voice. I freeze when I feel hurt or betrayed and pretend to look like I'm fully alive, unfazed. Each time a piece of my life is lost and what remains is artificial, fake, a fake girl, a painted backdrop, posed, as if everything was going on as it should.

Life Under Water

It's supposed to rain for nine days. Rain is very romantic in L.A. or Austin, where there was an attached garage and you could drive anywhere you wanted. Lightning flashed, illuminating the woods and the huge oak trees. There were French doors all across the back of the house where I could watch the drama into the wee hours with my trusty iPad on my lap and my dog and cat nearby for protection.

Here in New York it means one thing: I'm going to get wet. I'm starting to cough in anticipation. Amado left his keys on the table at the restaurant in South Street Seaport last night. We had just walked about five miles.

We took the ferry down to Wall Street, the water choppy, the boat pitching, the rain just starting. We got the keys, but Frannie was coughing and my feet were freezing. My $300 Cole Hahn raincoat turned out to not be impermeable. The wind was too strong for the umbrella.

I've become obsessed with the weather app on my phone. Is today looking like skin cancer or bronchitis?

Rain makes the flowers grow. It makes for big leafy trees and cleaner sidewalks, and in the summer, invites mosquitos. I need to walk the dog one more time tonight. I need to check the weather app. I won't eat anything that I don't already have. The black clouds are rapidly moving west. Only four more days to go.

It's Raining Cats And Dogs

Every day, from all sides, electronic, physical, telephonic, vacation, walking down the street I am confronted by animals needing rescuing, or humans soliciting on their behalf. I've been their advocate for many years, but the donations I make never seem to compete with the avalanche of animals being abused, abandoned, or neglected.

I see rescue stories daily on Facebook, but for every heartwarming rescue there's a horror story about how the animal came to need rescuing.

I have seen unspeakable cruelty on the pages of Facebook. I don't watch the videos or follow through, but the initial images sent by well-meaning friends haunt me still. I can't shake them.

My choir has been preached to. I get it. I donate monthly to SPCA, I gave Amado's bonus check to Austin Pets Alive, I have given to Amigos de Animales in San Miguel de Allende, but the deluge doesn't stop. There was that lab mix in San Miguel de Allende that followed us home to the hotel, and Amado took him on a wild goose chase to lose him.

There was that shepherd mix on Vieques that tried to get in the cab with me.

There was the puppy I found in a trash can in Sycamore Grove that my mother wouldn't let me take home, and somehow I look for the answer between helping a little and not knowing.

Like in the Edna St. Vincent Millay poem Renaissance, when awareness becomes so painful that she can't bear it and doesn't want to live, then she misses the feel of rain on her face, and the cycle starts again.

Period Four

When I was teaching at Lincoln High School, the students were put on tracks according to their reading level. The AP students were at the top, then level four just under them. I taught level three, which was my third period class, and level two, who were either the Chicano students who were slow readers or kids transitioning in from ESL. No one in level two read above a sixth-grade level.

I had these classes for a year for American Lit and Contemporary Comp. I had planned a good lesson that day. It wasn't like me to actually plan, but I was going to read the poem "Barbara" by Jacques Prévert, then have them write about anything that it brought up. "Barbara" was a vignette of love contrasted by the brutality of war.

I had the handouts of the poem and was waiting at the door, feeling the excitement and anticipation of an experience that was going to be rich. Third period came in restless and noisy, and wouldn't settle down. I tried to read the poem aloud and have them follow along, but it didn't work. They had no interest in it, it was chaos, I was trying to tame the forces of nature that didn't want to be tamed.

I gave up and had them do a grammar lesson out of their books, and peace was regained.

When my level two class came in, they asked me what was wrong, that I looked upset. I said it was nothing. They kept prodding me and I told them about the lesson that had failed in third period. They wanted to hear the poem, and I resisted then finally read it to them. They were fascinated, quiet, and totally engaged. Then I gave them time to write. The writing that they did was passionate and astounding.

I still have the piece a girl from Cambodia wrote—about coming home in the afternoon to a deserted neighborhood, her home empty, and not a living soul in sight. She finally heard a rustling in the bushes and it was her sister.

After some time she saw a figure approaching in the distance and realized finally as it got closer that it was her mother. This day left an imprint on me that has lasted over thirty years.

Root Beer

The first time I had a root beer float was at A&W in Vermont. We had just crossed over the border from Massachusetts, unless Massachusetts doesn't border on Vermont, then we passed over from somewhere else. I remember Anthony's cousin Joe and his wife Carol being with us, but I have no clue why they'd be with us because they live in New Jersey.

We always went to California to visit my parents for the summer. We were teachers and could do that, but this summer my parents said to meet them in Europe instead, so we spent almost all of our money buying tickets and reserving hotel rooms. By the time school got out, we had ten days left until our flight, $35 dollars in our bank account, and a Texaco gas card.

So we emptied our cupboards and put everything into our VW, emptied our refrigerator and put everything into an ice chest, packed our cockapoo, and headed north to New England.

That's how we happened to stop for a root beer float on that hot day in Vermont. I remember it as being breathtakingly fabulous. I never drank soda in any other form (except for a couple of Cuba libres in Mexico). I want one now. I also want those ten days back. It was a fabulous time. We slept on the beach in Cape Cod, stayed with Anthony's aunt in Pittsfield, smoked weed, and had dinner with my cousin in Newton. We then went to another cousin's for dinner somewhere on the Massachusetts coast and stayed for the weekend, and camped out in Maine, near the Canadian border. We were young and pretty and confident about the future. I remember being in love except for the time we got in a fight in the Berkshires. Anthony didn't have a sense of direction, and I wouldn't talk to him, so we kept driving in circles, me feeling smug and malevolent. Yes, I miss those days.

Musical Prodigy

My dad didn't play piano, so it's strange to me that my earliest memory of music was of him playing a piece by Mozart while I danced around a little hand-painted Mexican chair. I remember it being a thing that we did in our upstairs living room; the same blue shade as Frieda Kahlo's house in Coyocan.

Ours was a baby grand piano. My mother played, but not for fun. She only played when my father sang, in a throaty warble. He sang like Joseph Campbell spoke; Italian art songs, English folk songs, musical comedies, Opera, American folk songs, Negro spirituals. It was all there.

There was a record player, too. My brother had recorded different people; my grandpa singing a lullaby he wrote, my uncles, my brother; me.

I listened to recordings of my uncle, my brother, Marais and Miranda, Slim Gaillard, Stravinsky, Prokofiev. We didn't have a TV, so I read or listened to records.

I took piano lessons from Mrs. Ford who was related to John Anson Ford (the Ford Theater). I don't remember how, but my mother was very impressed with this. Mrs. Ford had dried rose petals in a glass canister and lived in Eagle Rock. I was impressed with the rose petals, but never practiced and faked it when I went to the lesson.

"I couldn't quite figure out these measures.... Would you play them for me?" And she would, and then I'd try to repeat what she'd done. It was pretty uncomfortable.

Ambushed

I keep thinking about the time Sherry and I were ambushed by boys as we walked home from Buchanan Street School up Avenue 50. We were on the sidewalk. I remember my lizard brain kicking in. Fight or flight. I always fought. I had older brothers. At home when I became furious, I didn't care if I was going to die. I fought.

I don't remember exactly what I did that day, but the image I'll never forget was Sherry slamming John Titus in the solar plexus with her plastic box purse. It was a full-armed swing that landed solidly. I remember the sound, and the boys who began their retreat.

I had always been impressed with Sherry. She was an all-out fighter. She later beat up Donna Adams in the bathroom in junior high. She was Irish. Maybe that had something to do with it.

Then there was my brother. He deserved what he got. He had dug into a tuna salad that I lovingly decorated with deviled eggs. He said I went after him with a knife. I remember a frying pan. I also remember throwing a roller skate at his head, but that was another incident. When the frying pan and knife didn't work I clawed him down his chest. He was bare-chested. He showed my dad, who told me that I wasn't a human being, I was an animal. A tiger would do something like that. I didn't like my dad's rage, or the fact that he didn't think I was a human being. I liked then and still like tigers; their fierceness, grace, and beauty.

The tiger showed up one last time when I was a kid, when I was spending the week with Eric Partlow in Idyllwild. He came as my companion, and we stayed in a little cabin in the woods off Strawberry Creek. He was a man at the age of ten. Mature beyond his years. He impressed Bess Haws who ran the guitar workshop so much that she told him he could take it for free, which left me alone.

When we came back, we decided to play catch. I was toward the bottom of the hill, and he was at the top. Every time I missed the ball I had to chase it down the hill and find it in the undergrowth. I suggested we switch sides and he didn't want to play anymore, so I did the tiger switch. I bloodied him down the front, which humiliated my father. Eric's father was his best friend, and I had done it again.

I have shown that side of me again. I don't have any Irish in me, God knows, but the eye of the tiger shows up when I've felt betrayed, mostly by a man, mostly in an intimate relationship. Maybe always in an intimate relationship. The tiger's gotten fat and lazy recently, but I suspect that it's still there, skulking somewhere, slouching toward Bethlehem to be born.

Crazy Howard

The year was 1965 and I was eighteen. I turned eighteen in the Ozarks, driving to New York from L.A. With my friend Lynn Roth and another girl whose VW we were in. I had to sit in the back all of the 3,200 miles, looking at the back of Lynn's head, while the two of them talked and enjoyed the scenery. The driver bought me a small tomato juice for my birthday.

I moved right in with Suzie, who was getting her BFA from NYU. She lived on Second Avenue and Tenth Street, second floor, looking out at the Saint Mark's Church. I was more mature than the other girls who were older and in college, and spent my time throwing lima beans out the window at the passersby. I was also pretty chunky, with a round face like a Cabbage Patch doll.

The apartment was set up like a whorehouse, with a long hallway down the middle leading to the small kitchen where Suzie and her roommates tore the plaster off the wall, leaving the red bricks. The kitchen was the gathering place, where Suzie, when she wasn't making ceramic bowls, was baking ceramic bread, and I'd make figurines out of the dough that didn't rise.

On either side of the hallway were the bedrooms, and each bedroom had a roommate, and her lover, except for mine and Suzie's. It was Suzie on her bed and me on a cot that tore my hair out when I caught it in the springs. When Suzie's heartthrob came over, I'd go to the kitchen and type and hum to myself to drown out the sex sounds that freaked me out.

Abbie Simpkin was a friend of Suzie's. I liked her too, and adopted her as a friend until she decided she was a lesbian and got drunk at a party and licked me on the nose. Abbie came over one day with Howard Cooper. He was perfect, and she didn't want him. He had beautiful Michelangelo eyes and red curly hair. He was also wearing jeans and a navy-blue t-shirt and had a great body (although at eighteen I wasn't aware of what that was doing to me). Some information had to have been exchanged, because I was going to go on a date with him and had nothing to wear. Having nothing to wear was not an affectation. It was literal. I had spent the weekend at a friend of my parents, Manny Manisoff and his family. I believe his wife was named Muriel and was one of the founders of Planned Parenthood. Muriel gave me a floral chiffon dress that I could barely zip up. It was sleeveless and had a fairly high round neck. I remember their home was on Long Island and was part of a tract, and it was a real house, separate from others, with wall-to-wall carpeting. Manny had something to do with theater, and spent most of the train ride back to Manhattan trying to convince me that I shouldn't go into acting. He sat next to me trying to dissuade me, talking about the payoffs, the corruption; that my brother had probably paid people off—all of this with a case of crippling halitosis. I was trying to be polite to my host, while withstanding his ideas and his breath.

My date was for that Saturday, and it was mid-week, so I took the floral chiffon dress to the tailor downstairs and asked him to please make the neck lower (just like in Westside Story). But, unlike Westside Story, when I went to pick it up that Saturday to try it on, the lining he used looked like it was taken from men's cotton boxer shorts. It was too late. I was pretty busty, and the lining showed.

Howard took me to Lincoln Center to see Kurosawa's Seven Samurai. This was so cool and so impressive.

We left the apartment, Howard and I, climbed down the stairs and tried to leave the building but there was a man sleeping in the doorway. I remember Howard asking him politely if we could get by, and he, the sleeping man, holding the door open for us with his foot.

Seven Samurai was long, and there was a lot of wonderful black and white cinematography, but what I remember most is the sound of bones cracking, and Toshiro Mifune's wonderful face.

Howard walked me home and kissed me good night. My knees buckled, and I would have fallen, but he held me up.

I don't think we went out again, but Howard was my main obsession for many years. I remember a line from a poem he wrote, or part of it:

It was Sophie on the _____ ground was all there was that day.

I asked Howard who his favorite poet was and he said, "Yeats". "Oh! That's how you pronounce it," I said. "I always thought it was pronounced 'Yeets' and I always confused him with Keats!"

The look he gave me sent me immediately to a bookstore to buy Palgraves Golden Treasury, and I was determined to read every poem in the thousand-something pages.

I eventually got my own bedroom in the whorehouse and I proceeded to paint it white with a sponge. I was making $25 a week at Barnes & Noble and couldn't afford luxuries like brushes.

There was no electricity in that room, so I slogged through the Treasury by candlelight. When I moved back to California, my dad used to sit in the garden with me and we finished the book, taking turns reading, and marking each poem with a grading system I devised.

I remember also comparing growing up in L.A. with growing up in New York City. I said that instead of living with a dog with floppy ears you had a drunk peeing in the gutter. He thought it was hilarious, and used a literary term for the comparison I made. I realized again that I had done something painfully naive, and I was hopeless. Howard could never love me; but I kept trying.

Camels

What makes me angriest is my children or Amado. I look at the news and I have a special compartment for that rage; that overwhelming rage and despair coupled with impotence, and it sits in a bubble somewhere, behind plastic, the whole package, like the meat at Ralph's at the end of the day. The fat gets turned into soap to clean us (of our sins). I read that sin was originally an archery term; that we missed the mark. I don't know what they do with the spoiled meat. It's the waste of a life, but the bottom line is profit. I guess that's the bottom line for everything in this society.

Profit is a funny word. Whose profit? Someone's finances. Depression, they say, is rage turned inward. I like both kinds.

I wish they'd feed Christians to lions again. Not all Christians, of course, just the religious Right. False Christians. Those who forgot what Jesus's teachings were about: loving thy neighbor as thyself, turning the other cheek, and getting a camel through the eye of a needle. It seems that the whole world is hell-bent on getting those damn camels through the eye of a needle.

Rudeman

I was in my early twenties and flying to New York. To my left was an attractive and fascinating man with black curly hair and intelligent eyes. I think he mentioned his girlfriend a dozen times on that flight. I didn't have the capacity to say at that age, "I know you have a girlfriend. I don't have any designs on you nor ideas of attachment. I'm not trying to woo you or get in your pants. I'm merely trying to pass the time on the plane."

I don't remember what it was about him that was smart and rude, but it did make the time go by, and when we landed in New York I was relieved that I wouldn't have to see him again.

Many months later I was registering for classes at Cal State L.A. The sun was strong and the line was long. Who should walk by but Rudeman. Our eyes met and we chatted for a few minutes. I don't remember what we spoke about, but it was interesting and I felt slightly offended when he left. I remember the feeling well, but not the context. It felt like I wasn't good enough. That he was superior. That I would have liked him if he gave me a chance, but he didn't. And when he left, I thought, God, I'm glad that's over.

Many months later I had rented a little guest house near L.A.C.C. I was walking to school on Monroe, and there were many little California bungalows, with drying student lawns, cracked porches, and graying paint. A man was standing out in his frontyard. He had dark curly hair and a beard. He walked up to me, world-weary, and yes, it was Rudeman.

We talked a bit and I continued on to class.

By now I had accepted him, so like in spiritual parables, once I accepted him I never saw him again.

Having The Relatives Over

Anthony and I were living on Bergen Avenue in Jersey City in a fourth-floor walk-up while he was finishing his BA-teaching credential. I went to a clinic to get an IUD put in. I must have been the last patient of the day, because I remember them telling me that I had to get off the table, because they were leaving. The problem was I couldn't get off the table. When they got me up, I couldn't walk, which really annoyed them because it was time to go home.

Someone who worked there got me into her car. I don't remember how, but they dumped me in front of my apartment building. I got to the front door and onto a step, but couldn't climb. Somehow Anthony found me there and helped me up the four flights. When he grasped the shape I was in, he gave me some of his stash, Cibas, which was a type of sleeping pill, Doriden, and codine cough syrup.

Soon I was feeling fine and able to start preparing dinner. My uncle and aunt showed up, and I took out the dinner. I was delighted to see them, and sitting around the table, with my first relatives and the only relatives that came to visit, my head kept lowering to the table. It was just that comfortable there on the table. I knew somehow that this was rude, but couldn´t say so, and couldn't keep upright.

I remember my head snapping up, like those hollow-eyed men on the F train, but I didn't care. I did care, however, when I brought out the cauliflower au gratin in a casserole dish and there was a caterpillar on top, dead, like a melted birthday candle.

I hope we had a nice dessert for them and that the rest of the dinner was charming. I don't think they ever ate at our place again. I can't imagine why. It was better going to their place anyway. Ruth had the most delightful hors d'oeuvres, like apricots with cream cheese and nuts, and baked chicken with a crunchy cornflake crust. It was all presented very nicely, and my uncle Mitch would fall asleep on the floor.

Ice Cream And Hannah As A Deposit

Part I
Dad was an art teacher at John Adams Junior High School, but when he was called up before the Senate committee under Joe McCarthy and questioned and asked to name names and he refused, he got fired. They fired him just before Christmas, when I was five. His statement in the papers (and his photo was all over the papers) was, "I think it's a hell of a thing to do just before Christmas". They let him keep his job long enough to finish the Christmas assembly, though, because they didn't have anyone else to do it.

Dad had used an African-American Madonna in the John Adams Christmas Pageant that year, and when the L.A. times heard that, they refused to do the article. Dad and his students had made paper-stained glass windows to decorate the main building that he talked about the rest of his life. He was so proud.

For the rest of his life he had to struggle to keep a job. He'd lie about his experience, and get experience while they found out he didn't know what he was doing. Then he'd get fired again and start a new job with a little more experience. He was now working as a draftsman. This all was fine with me, though, because each time he got a new job I'd get an ice cream cone from Curries, on Riverside Drive. Peppermint Stick. Always, and it was a 'mile-high cone' shaped like a wedge. It was special.

Part II
I was a single parent for fourteen years, and it was a struggle, although I enjoyed life, and I sometimes enjoyed the struggle. My kids weren't always thrilled, though. I remember when Hannah was about twelve, I took her shopping (teachers get paid once a month) and we loaded the

cart, and I mean it was top heavy! When we got to the cashier and she rang everything up I realized I had forgotten my check book, so I left Hannah as a deposit with the groceries and drove home about 80 mph to get it. I don't think I even had the psychic energy to beat myself up that time, but Hannah was weary of having that kind of mother, and it was obvious on her face when I arrived, triumphant, check book in hand.

The Interview

It had been a couple of years since I got my master's degree in writing when I heard Ventura College had a full-time position for an English teacher. I sent in my resume and lined up an interview. I was about forty and had a perfect dress that I had bought for a TV appearance with two lines in some prank show that didn't do too well.

The dress was a soft, dusty-pink silk shirt waist with a button-down front and self-tying belt. I looked perfect. I had planned my sample lesson plan. I felt confident. It was a foolproof lesson. I had reviewed the questions they were going to ask me and I was well greased, honed, and ready to show them my stuff. I had been teaching all of my adult life and had a couple of years of community college teaching under my belt.

This job would take me away from the San Fernando Valley and away from L.A., into a fresh new beachy setting. I could feel the cool breeze fluttering my lovely mid-calf prudent skirt as I sauntered across the shady lawn to the room where I met the panel of Academicians who were going to be my pupils for the lesson.

I taught them how to cluster and map ideas for a perfectly crafted foolproof college essay.

I answered their questions with poise and maturity. I was feeling fine. I had control, but was not bossy; humble yet confident. At the end of the session one of the professors raised his hand, and I called on him, my hands still clasped around the hand-out materials that I had plenty of.

"If you were to teach a literature class, what would you teach?" he asked.

I thought about his question, gave it some time, and opened my lips to respond, but nothing came out. I couldn't think of any literature. I couldn't think of a short story, a play, a novel, a biography, I couldn't think of a comic book, a poem or a TV show. I went completely blank.

I knew I was dying there; that not even the perfect dress could save me.

They thanked me and I left. I sat in my car before I drove home, hitting my head on the steering wheel. I had been a voracious reader all my life, and anxiety came in from somewhere hidden, to attack me and turn me into an idiot. I never heard from them, of course. I didn't call them. D. H. Lawrence. Shakespeare. Dylan Thomas; Dostoyevsky; Tolstoy. Arnold Wesker, Annie Dillard, Nathaniel West. Oh, what the hell. It was a nice dress, though.

My Holiday

My favorite holiday is my birthday, June 24th. It doesn't have the glitz and traditions of Christmas, or the history and soul of Jewish holidays. It doesn't have bunnies, chocolates or green grass like Easter, or the sinister masks and child princesses of Halloween. But the day is indisputably mine, without expectations, traditions or the impingement of trappings. It's a blank canvas, all mine, with whatever palate I choose.

The numbers thrill me. Whenever the clock says 6:24, I feel a glow, as if it were greeting me; our shared secret. I'm grateful to the clock. I favor number 24: the 24th psalm, Shakespeare's 24th sonnet, the soccer player with a 24 on his jersey; it always winks at me, salutes me.

Yesterday was my day. I just wanted a handful of people over—no gifts, no dressing up, no fuss—just hummus and peppers. It often starts like this. Then I start wanting a few good friends over. It ends up with me inviting people on the elevator; people on my floor. As my birthday approaches, they all seem like good friends. I get lost serving the hummus. I always forget something. We end up getting pizza. It's perfect. The buzz of conversation, blending perfectly; no one feeling left out stays with me.

People leave, then tell me how great my dog and cat are, how Frannie was licking the cat's ear. The baby was running around on her newfound legs, vocalizing for anyone wanting to harmonize. I made it through a tough year, I'm still me, and I'm still grateful to be alive, and that's something to celebrate.

Edna Is A Charming Girl

Dedicated to Julie Davey, who showed me that writing can heal

There I was, waiting for my improv class to start, a Boomer awash in a sea of Millennials. Suddenly the door opened and a new student walked in. Little did I know my life was about to change. Her scenes were magical, and I noticed she was unafraid of sounding weird or child-like. I wanted to know this person, so after a few weeks I asked if she would be interested in going out after class and having a late-night dessert at The House of Pies, a nearby Hollywood landmark. We bonded over chocolate cream pie, a bear claw, and strong coffee. And that's how Deborah and I met.

A few months later, Bonnie joined the class (as did Bonnie's husband, Amado, and dog, Frannie). Deborah knew Bonnie from another class, and she introduced me. We did scenes together, and I knew Bonnie had a creative streak a mile long. She has a combination of innocence and street smarts that is irresistible. I didn't know we shared an ethnic bond and a place of origin in Los Angeles until much later, when she moved to the East Coast.

Deborah, Bonnie, and I are different yet so similar. It is uncanny how our life experiences have diverged on the surface, but our underlying values and way of looking at the world have a rock-solid unity. I can't imagine my life without these two wonderful ladies.

Butting In

It's 3:00 pm and I'm meeting my improv friend for a drink at Peet's Coffee in East Pasadena. It's a sweltering August day, so everyone is inside doing their coffee-house thing. I get there first and scope out the seating situation: all of the tables for two are taken, and there's a young man at a table for four, staring at his phone.

I don't like to invade people's space. If this were Europe, no one would think twice about me sitting at their table. But this is Los Angeles and people are ferociously protective of their caffeinated territory. I wait in line, considering the etiquette of it all, when a woman around my age gets her drink, walks up to phone-man and asks him if she can sit at his table. She doesn't really ask per se but rather mumbles something and sits down.

Crap! I knew I should have asked phone-guy if I could join him. Mumble-lady doesn't seem to have any qualms about coffee shop propriety. My friend specifically does not want to sit outside, and I totally agree. I am kicking myself. Why did I have to be so damn polite? Now I'm in a pickle because we absolutely cannot sit outside.

The table for four now has two occupants. There are no other tables that seat four. I know what I have to do. I walk over to the table, look at phone-guy and say, "I guess this is the communal table?" in my most innocent voice. Phone-guy mumbles something like, "Oh, sure," and butt-in lady just glares at me. Then, looking toward the back of the shop, she motions with her hand to a man at a table for two and says, "Maybe that man will let you sit at his table."

Now I'm pissed. As Jerry Ohrbach says to Patrick Swayze in Dirty Dancing, "No one puts Baby in the corner."

Butt-in lady has thrown down the gauntlet, and I refuse to let her lower my status and raise hers. I pull on my big-girl panties, look down at her and say, very sweetly, "I'm meeting a friend so I need two spaces," and then plop myself down in between her and phone-man.

Butt-in lady does a slow burn, and I am chortling inside. Try to lower my status, will you? No effing way.

I sit and check my phone while she tries to expand her territory by spreading out her book, phone, coffee, and muffin. I don't give an inch.

Then phone-guy looks up and says, "Well, if I don't go to the gym now I'll never go." He promptly gets up and leaves. Butt-in lady and I dig our trenches, drawing a bitter Maginot Line on the tabletop.

Finally my friend shows, gets her drink, and joins me at the table. We talk about auditions, plays, other improv friends, and catch up in general. Butt-in lady pretends to ignore us but I know she is listening to every word. Ten minutes later she gathers her book, cup, and crumbs, and stands.

I flash her a teeth-blazing smile and, dripping with sincerity, say, "THANK you SO much for allowing us to sit at your table. That was SO kind of you. You have a wonderful afternoon, now!"

Butt-in lady is confused; she gives me a startled look, grabs her stuff and shuffles out of the store.

I explain to my friend what transpired before she arrived, and she gives me a high-five and a "You-go-girl." We talk, gesticulate, laugh, conspire, and have a great time.

I leave Peet's with a wee bit of a smirk, and a spring in my step, despite the heat.

How I Retired

The spirit world made me retire.

I was already unhappy with my job as a senior systems analyst at a large medical research facility. My supervisor had a PhD in epidemiology and had no business supervising anyone. I came from a human resources background and could see that she was totally miscast in the role. I was assigned to do what amounted to data entry into a system that I knew would never see the light of day.

I was stuck in a dead-end situation, but I had not yet consciously decided to leave.

Sometime later I went with friends to a psychic, who happened to be a friend of a friend. Eventually she asked if we wanted to try the Ouija board and we all jumped at the chance. Who knew what we'd uncover? I asked Ouija which year I would retire, and it spelled out the following year. Crap, I wasn't sure I could last that long.

Two months later, on Super Bowl Sunday, my friend was running her first vision board workshop, where you cut out pictures and words from magazines and then assemble them on a large poster board. It's supposed to represent important things about who you are and what you want in life. I was pissed that it was on Super Bowl Sunday but I wanted to support my friend, so I went.

Cutting out pictures was fun, I have to admit. Almost as much fun as playing with paper dolls as a child.

When everyone assembled their vision boards, we shared our designs. After my presentation, my friend said, "Edna, you didn't put one thing about work on your board," and I replied, "Why should I? I hate my job!"

It was the first time that thought had come into my consciousness, and I said it with such vehemence it shocked me.

Four weeks later, Miss PhD Supervisor gave me my annual review. She did everything wrong you can do in a review, and I was so frustrated and angry I almost burst into tears in her office. I had to take a walk around the grounds for an hour, I was so angry and frustrated.

The next day I made an appointment to see her, sat down and handed her a memo with one sentence: "This is to inform you that I am resigning effective March 17." Miss PhD was floored and could not understand why I was leaving. She even tried to convince me to stay.

The last two weeks at the job were the best weeks I ever spent there. I had finally listened to my inner vision and the cosmic helpers whispering at me to follow my own path.

He Laughs Best Who Laughs Last

I believe this is a variation of "He who laughs last, lasts best" and "Revenge is sweet" and "Revenge is a dish best served cold."

I never understood the last one. Why is revenge best if it's cold? I like cold food. For god's sake, ice cream is cold. I never think, "I'd like to get revenge on X. I know, I'll send them a Baskin-Robbins ice cream cake"! Or cold pizza. Who came up with this?

I am not an outwardly vengeful person. I don't harbor violent thoughts on those who have wronged me. Well, ok, there was that awful boss. But I never took any action. It stayed, simmering in some internal organ where I paid a health cost instead.

I don't do that anymore—think vengeful thoughts. Except for people who cause political insanity (insert name here) or are cruel to animals.

There was one time, though, when I got such a sweet (harmless) revenge.

I was the assistant human resources manager at the downtown L.A. corporate headquarters of a major retailer. He was the vice president of human resources. He was tall, lean, and sort of handsome in an effete way. He was a snob and favored himself a highly-cultured Francophile. At Christmas, he would invite his management colleagues (never the lower classes) to his home in the Los Feliz hills near the Greek theater, where he and his thin, cultured French wife would formally entertain.

I was not invited, but my colleague who went reported back that it was the stuffiest party she'd ever been to, and she made her exit as soon as was politically acceptable.

Think Louis Jourdan in Gigi.

I finally left that job, and two years later I was at a preview of antique

French furniture at Butterfield's auction house on Sunset Boulevard. Across the room I spied someone familiar. Sure enough, it was Louis Jourdan from my old job. My first instinct was to avoid him, but then a little voice inside said, "Hey, let's have a little fun."

I approached Louis, and when he turned toward me I said, "Hello, there! Good to see you again." Now that was mean, because I knew he wouldn't necessarily remember a lower-status former employee. But he did seem to recognize me a little, because he said, hesitantly, "Oh yes, hello, how are you? Good to see you again."

This was bullshit, of course, but I did enjoy seeing him squirm. His brain was frantically trying to come up with my name but was coming up with vapors. His discomfort was comforting.

And then it happened. He asked, "Are you interested in any of the pieces in the auction?"

I waited a few delicious seconds, then answered: "Oh, no, I have a few pieces I'm selling. Those three chairs you were just looking at."

Mr. Jourdan, totally confused at this assault on his world order, managed to mumble, "Oh, yes, yes, well that's very good." He turned and slowly walked away in a mental haze.

Karma is a dish best served cold.

Growing Taller Than Trees

I'm a big fan of shade. Not throwing shade, being in the shade.

Just like every SoCal kid, in the summer I wanted to sport a perfect tan. I would go downstairs to the backyard, spread out my colorful beach towel, slather myself with Coppertone ("Don't be a Paleface!"), assume the "snow angel" position, and bake in the sun.

After days of baking, I was not tan. A more accurate description would be "painfully burnt to a crisp".

My aunt swore by Heinz white vinegar as an antidote to sunburn. Actually, she used vinegar as an antidote to most everything, from bug bites to scrapes and indigestion. She would come home from a Sunday at the beach and immediately douse herself in vinegar and invite me to do the same. It never helped, and I wound up smelling like salad dressing.

Eventually I learned that my skin progressed quickly from pale to lobster red, skipping over the tanning part completely. From that point on, I recognized that shade was my new best friend.

I became the friend who couldn't go to the beach without fully covering up, the one who brought the industrial-strength umbrella, who wouldn't go on walks without her safari hat, water bottle, or additional sunblock (just in case), who needed to stop and rest in the shade while the others went their merry way.

F*ck them.

Trees are my friends. They give me oxygen and shade, and I give them water and good vibes. It works.

Two weeks ago we had a freak monsoon episode and the temperature rocketed to 119 degrees. That's the hottest day on record here since anyone cared to measure the weather. I hunkered down and survived. A week later I was looking out the bedroom window and saw my beloved sequoias, and all I saw were brown fronds. They had burnt in the blistering heat.

I almost burst into tears. I tried to tell myself that I couldn't control the weather, maybe they would bounce back, not to let my emotions get the best of me, it could have been worse, blah blah blah.

It was like my best friend had died.

So, if I grew taller than trees, I could never experience their shade ever again, and that thought is unbearable.

Good Old Boys

After eleven years as a software engineer with the county, I decided to go back into private industry. I got a job as a systems analyst with a company that developed software for the auto repair industry. I was one of a few female IT employees; management was totally male.

I enjoyed the first year with the company, writing technical manuals and learning about the world of auto repair. I did well, and at the time of my annual review my manager promoted me to senior systems analyst. I was making good money, appreciated by my boss, and my future was looking up. Then my department hired two more analysts, and the manager asked if I would be interested in supervising them. I was flattered, but cautious; I had had a horrible experience as a supervisor in a previous job and vowed never to do it again. My boss was persistent, and I finally said yes.

Things devolved. The new male analyst quickly made it known that he should be the supervisor because he was a man. Six months later he filed a complaint with HR about me and returned to Pakistan. The new female analyst had been hired over my objections; she had no experience but was pretty. After a few weeks I realized she had little technical writing skills, and she spent most of her time making friends and looking pretty. I wound up redoing most of her work, in addition to my own. After months of this, I brought this up to my manager, who agreed we should get her on disciplinary action. Four months later, she was let go for basic incompetence. Little did I know that I had created internal enemies.

One of the management perks at this company was going to the Comdex convention in Las Vegas, where all the latest in computer and electronic gadgetry was on display. My manager and I decided to drive together. Before he became my manager, he had been a friend and colleague of mine, so it was a natural choice. We liked each other, but strictly as colleagues and professionals.

A few weeks after Comdex, the manager called me into his office, closed the door and told me that many in our department were unhappy with the female analyst's firing, and they blamed me for pushing her out. They wanted a meeting to air their grievances. The manager told me to go to this meeting, he would be the facilitator, and I was to be totally silent, no matter what happened.

I had no idea I was stepping into a den of vipers. One guy accused me of bullying the former female analyst. Others expressed their displeasure at how strict I was, that I was cold and unfeeling, and I was unfair and a lousy supervisor to boot. The clincher came when a younger female employee stood up and accused me of having an affair with the manager and using my favored status to my advantage.

I sat there and said nothing, as the manager had directed. Inside, I was angry and indignant. As for the affair accusation, it was so shocking on one hand, and silly on the other, but the mob mentality at that meeting left me unsure of my professional abilities. Is this the way I came over to these people, these vindictive, mean-spirited, lying people?

A few weeks later, the Friday before Thanksgiving week, the HR manager showed up in my cubicle and asked if I would come to her office. There she told me that the company was experiencing financial difficulties and they would have to lay me off. I had to go back to my cubicle, get my purse, return to her office, and then be escorted out by security staff. My manager had seen me get my purse; he said nothing, went into his office and closed the door.

It took me weeks to come to grips with the trauma of losing my job, the anger and humiliation, and the sense that I had done something wrong, even though I knew I hadn't.

They spoke a language that was foreign to me, a language I couldn't understand and definitely didn't want to learn.

Genealogy

I don't know you. I don't even know your names. I don't know what you looked like, what your favorite color was, what foods you liked to eat. I don't know how you married your husbands/wives, although it's a good guess they were arranged. Where did you live? Were you religious? Did you wear a wig when you got married?

Since my family never talked about life in the Old Country, I grew up believing that my history began in Massachusetts and most of it occurred in Los Angeles. I knew only one grandparent, my mother's mother. And she lived next door, so she was someone I knew well.

Or did I? I have no idea what her favorite anything was. She even changed her name, form Leyka to Lena, so much more American. You were the only one who fought for me, even just a little. You got my parents to let me have the teenager cat who showed up on our doorstep when I was eight. Thank you thank you, you have no idea how much I loved Tiger. Tiger was my friend.

I learned from a distant cousin just recently that you came to Ellis Island with your four girls, twelve years after your husband left for the US. I didn't know you were sick and were detained at a hospital for two days. You must have recovered enough to stay. It's so tenuous; what would our lives have been like if you were sent back to Russia and my mother grew up motherless? Would I have been born?

And the others. Genealogy is a blessing and a curse. It answers some questions, but reveals things you didn't really want to know. Like how my very existence depended on my grandfather coming here and sending for my grandmother twelve years later. The same with my father's father.

I know now that I must have had many relatives who stayed behind, and then they were rounded up in the forests and shot, falling into mass graves.

I don't know you. But you are in me. I feel it.

"May their memory be a blessing."

Distraction

Sometimes I feel frightened, then overwhelmed, then panicked. If it's a good day, my adult makes an attempt to calm me down, using common-sense logic mixed with mantras like, "It could be so much worse" and "No one I know is in the hospital." Sometimes it works, sometimes it doesn't. I have also learned that distraction is a fine tool in our modern world; it's not a waste of time, it's downright patriotic and economically sound. Psych wards cost money and create anxiety for loved ones.

And that, my friends, is why I drive myself down to our local Trader Joe's. Sometimes it's on the way, and sometimes it's not. Sometimes I actually need to buy some items, and sometimes I buy a default banana, or organic free-trade dark chocolate. Hell, I don't drink or do drugs.

I have come to the conclusion that the free food and coffee samples at Trader Joe's are magical, put on this earth by a kind and gentle force that understands panic and fear. At least I hope so.

And so there I was, three days ago, entering my temple of temptation and redemption. After a moment of refreshment from the strong air conditioning, I approached the flower aisle for the traditional receiving of my mother's celestial blessing through ritual sniffs, letting the pungent smell take me back to my childhood. On my way to the flowery chapel, I noticed a cart full of items, with a woman's purse in the front, but with no woman attached.

I like to think I'm a helpful person, so I looked for the cart owner. I asked another woman in the flower section if the cart was hers, but she said no, she thought it belonged to the young girl looking at the display outside.

My first reaction was, "Idiot! Someone's going to steal your purse," but I decided to watch over her cart until she returned. Sure enough, a minute later, Ms. Cart Owner appeared: mid-twenties, dressed in all black, with thick black eye liner and face piercings.

I approached. "I've been watching your cart. You shouldn't leave your cart with your purse in it, it's not safe." I thought I was being helpful. Her face expressed many emotions, but the one she acted on was snark.

"Don't worry, I can take care of myself!" she huffed, and made a beeline to checkout. I expected maybe a "Thank you for caring" or even an "OK, thanks." I felt strange, like I had done something wrong. Why was she so rude? I was only trying to help.

She ruined my happy place. I felt maligned. I bought my banana and left. I had to do a little cleansing ritual in my car to get her anger off of me. The nerve of her!

Now I have had a few days to think about it, and all I can feel for this young woman is sadness. For her need of bravada. For her need to show the world she could survive without help, without caring, without community, without love. Who or what did you fear, that you had to fight back against a stranger concerned for your safety?

I wanted a distraction, just not that one. Sometimes spirit gives you what you need, not what you want.

Well, no one I know is in the hospital.

Censored Homework

The first time I encountered homework was in the sixth grade, in the class of my most beloved teacher, Miss Delworth. Every day she gave us a mimeographed sheet with arithmetic problems: multiplication with decimal numbers, long division to eight places out, word problems that anticipated beginning algebra, and sometimes a bonus question about pop culture. It never had anything to do with math—it was just a joke to blow off mental steam.

We could work on the problems in our spare time in class or take them home to turn in the next day. Miss Delworth gave each of us a homemade notebook consisting of two sheets of heavy, gray construction paper and three golden brads. After completing a sheet of math problems, we got to punch it with the three-hole punch and secure it in the notebook. Such a rewarding experience. Each week, my notebook grew and grew, as did my confidence in my math abilities.

Every day at three o'clock I neatened my desk, gathered my purse, lunch bag, and arithmetic notebook, and walked home. My favorite TV show came on around that time: The Soupy Sales Show, with Soupy and his wacky gang of puppets: White Fang, Black Tooth, and, of course, Pookie the Lion. Soupy's show was full of slapstick humor, wild puns, surprise guests, and silly conversations with his puppets.

Sometimes I did my math homework while watching Soupy, and I would doodle all around the edges of my notebook. Maybe I'd draw White Fang's paw in one corner, write out Black Tooth's amorous come-ons next to an equation, sketch an impromptu picture of Pookie, etc. I never showed my homework to anyone else, so what did it matter?

Well, it mattered. One day Miss Delworth said to the class, "It's time for open house and I want to show your parents all of your arithmetic work, so please get your notebooks organized and ready to turn in tomorrow. Then I will have them available for the open house, and your work will be on display for everyone to see."

I felt the room spin. My head was hot and my stomach was churning. It was the end of the world. No one could see my notebook with all of my stupid Soupy Sales doodles. I felt so frightened and humiliated. I could not be found out! I had messed up.

I decided the only way to save myself was to go through each page in the notebook and erase all of my creative musings. Luckily they were in pencil, and even better, I had my trusty Pink Pearl eraser close at hand. I spent that evening erasing all art, puns, jokes, and other creative takes on the show sprinkled through most of the pages. It took what seemed like hours, and when I was finished not only did my hands ache from the erasing, but my psyche ached from the eradication of the "me-ness" in my work.

The notebook was ready for prime time—proper, prepared, and bland as could be. I had wiped myself off the pages for fear of appearing different or weird.

Miss Delworth gave me an A+ for the open-house version of the notebook.

Looking back today, I wish I had thrown caution to the wind and kept the notebook as it was, with all the cleverness and the artwork and the fun and the wit intact.

C'mon, Pookie, let's go get a mocha latte.

Bugs In Your Salad

I was a college senior majoring in Art History at UCLA and working twenty hours per week at the Getty Museum in Malibu. That's where I met Tom, a friend of the museum director. Tom was a nice guy and I think he fancied me, but I always considered him just a friendly work pal.

One day Tom told me about a great place near the beach where the pizza was rocking it. It wasn't fancy, Tom said, but the food was great. "It's called Chez Puce. That's French for 'House of the Flea'." He mentioned the owners were a married couple, their last name was Puce, the wife was chef, and her husband was the host and waiter.

Maybe that was Tom's way of asking me out, but I didn't bite. Instead, I told some friends about the restaurant and they were enthusiastic about a visit, so that Saturday night I found myself at Chez Puce, a small, cozy place with ruffled white curtains and tables covered with blue and white checked cloths. The lighting was romantic: wine bottles with candles dribbling long strands of wax down the sides. Very chic.

Monsieur Puce's first name was Robert; of course he pronounced it "Row-bear". He sat us at a table for six, and made sure to pull out the chairs for les mademoiselles. Menus were produced with a flourish. Robert was spreading it thick, and I was loving every moment of this Folies Bergère show, starring the one and only "Row-bear".

Meanwhile, Madame Puce sulked in the background, waiting for the order, giving her husband the evil eye when he got too close to the girls.

Chez Puce was not a French restaurant, it was more of a college pizza joint. So, of course, we ordered enough pizzas to feed six hungry students. Robert shouted the order to his wife, and after some heated words, she stalked into the kitchen.

Fifteen minutes later, Robert came out with our order and cut the pizzas with the precision of a Moulin Rouge dancer. I took a piece, but after a few bites I could tell something was wrong. It was very stringy, and not from the mozzarella cheese. I called Robert over, expressed my concern, and waited. He cocked his head and looked at the triangular piece from all angles, all the while muttering in French. Finally he took the slice with him to the kitchen, where I heard loud voices and what must have been French expletives. Then silence.

Madame Puce and Robert exited the kitchen and approached our table. Robert was carrying a floor mop in his hand, like a spear. He said, with a matter-of-fact-delivery, "Oh, it's ok, it's just pieces of the mop in the pizza." And Mr. and Mrs. stood there, a united front. I said, "But I can't eat this, it has pieces of MOP in it!" With a straight face, Madame Puce replied, "It is no problem. The mop is clean." And she left the table, shaking her head, as if to say, "What is wrong with these silly Americans."

We were so shocked we didn't know what to do. Finally we decided to just pay the bill and go. When a flea tells you a mop in your pizza is no problem, it's definitely time to call it an evening.

No Joke

At age eight I started to gain weight. I have theories on why, but it's hard to know exactly what was triggering my dependence on food. For the next eight years my identity at school was Edna the Smart Fat Girl (or maybe the other way around).

Every magazine, TV show, and movie reminded me that I was unattractive, unwanted, and worthless. Boys would never want me, that's for sure. By the time I was 15, I wore a junior size 15. To put that into perspective, most stores carried junior sizes up to 13, so I had to shop in misses' size 16 or 18. Misses' were for older women with jobs and families, not swinging teens who shopped only in the junior department. There was even a chain of stores called the 3-5-7 Shop that carried adorable clothes for teens, but I was four sizes too big to fit into their biggest size 7.

In my first semester of high school I took a music appreciation class, and the teacher required us to attend at least three classical concerts of our choice. I asked my friend Steve Klein if he would go with me to the Music Center downtown. The Music Center had only been opened for a couple of years, and it was considered very special and high-end, a "dress up" kind of place. Steve said yes, so all I needed was an appropriate dress.

One Sunday my family went to Sears on Pico Boulevard. The front doors opened to the candy department, and my memory of freshly buttered Sears popcorn is seared in my brain. I went to the junior department, not very optimistic, but lo and behold they carried a few size 15s, and there was a long-sleeved A-line dress checked in a lovely sky-blue and white with a Peter Pan collar and satin blue ribbon.

I couldn't believe it—it fit! My mother actually bought it for me. I felt almost desirable in it. Almost. It was still me in the size 15 dress, after all.

The night of the concert, Steve picked me up (in a suit!) and, since he had his license, drove me to the Music Center. I was painfully aware of the other concertgoers, especially the glamorous women in their black sequin tops and high heels. Steve handed our tickets to one of the two good-looking male ushers, who looked at Steve, then at me, and said to Steve, "You're a lucky man, sir!"

Steve replied something nondescript, like, "Oh, yeah."

The two ushers exchanged a smirk and an eyeroll. I felt so embarrassed and humiliated, but also that they had a right to smirk and joke, because I was a joke after all.

Steve said he enjoyed the music; I don't think I heard a note of it.

Choose Me

I vividly remember a moment of pure joy when I was in the third grade. It was so long ago, yet I still get goose bumps when I think about it.

We are in class, sitting at our long communal tables that serve as desks. A visitor enters the room. I recognize her as Miss Abel, the music teacher. My teacher, Miss Plough, interrupts her lesson and, clapping her hands briskly, announces, "Attention, children! Miss Abel is here to select students to sing in the school chorus. She will give you a song to sing. If she pats you on the shoulder as she walks by, that means you have been chosen. If that happens, come to the front of the class and stand quietly."

I can't believe my ears. Here is a chance for me to sing in the school chorus! I can make music with the other children, with Miss Abel leading us. The thought fills me with such excitement I can hardly sit still. Silently, I start to pray—"Please, please, please choose me. Please, please, please, I want to sing. Please, please, please."

We start our trial song. I watch Miss Abel's every movement with intense interest. When she touches a child's shoulder, it is as though she has turned Cinderella from the servant girl into the princess.

She starts to come down my aisle. "Please, oh please," I plead with whoever or whatever has the power to intercede on my behalf with Miss Abel. Finally, she passes and I feel the slightest tap on my shoulder. Did I imagine it, or is it real? I look up at Miss Abel. She smiles at me and whispers, "Yes."

I want to run and scream with a sense of delicious, intense joy. I have been chosen. I am special.

As an adult, I have sung in prominent choral groups and count my blessings to participate. But nothing comes close to capturing the joy of that moment, so long ago, when Miss Abel gave me my voice.

No Return Policy

Linda Ligrano was my best friend in the sixth grade at Laurel School in West Hollywood. We talked about everything happening in our world. Bozo the Clown was popular, and we would watch it every day after school, then talk about it the next day on the playground. Bozo had a live studio audience of kids our age. In between filmed material, Bozo would make silly jokes and then choose kids to come on stage and play games for prizes.

I was ten years old and I loved Bozo. He was my after-school friend. I longed to be in the audience and, should I even hope, play a game and win a fantastic prize? I knew he filmed the show live because of the kids in the bleachers. How could I become a Bozo kid?

Bozo was on KTTV Channel 5 in Los Angeles. I looked up KTTV in the Yellow Pages and found the address on Sunset Boulevard in Hollywood. I wrote to Bozo and asked for tickets to the show. A few weeks later the mailman deposited an important looking manila letter. Bozo had delivered!

I was so excited! Somehow, I got my father to agree to drive me to the show (he was the only one in the family who drove). The next day I basically plowed into Linda Ligrano on the playground and showed her the tickets and asked if she wanted to come with me. She did! Oh this was going to be SO MUCH FUN!

I never went anywhere after school or had friends over, so this was an incredibly big deal. I counted down the days. Finally, Linda and I were sitting in the Bozo bleachers and there he was! All us kids were screaming and laughing, and nothing else mattered in the world.

Then the big moment came. "Whoa Nellie, kids, who wants to play a game and win a fabulous prize?" Oh me me me me me me! I waved my arm until it practically dislocated, then I heard Bozo say, "You! Come on up!" and I knew he had picked me. I started to get up, but then I saw Linda bound up and go on stage.

No no no no no no no! This was all wrong, he chose the wrong girl! It was me he wanted, not Linda! I found the address, I wrote the letter, I got the tickets, I arranged transportation, me me me! What right did Linda have to play the game and win a fabulous prize?

So Linda played the game, lost, and wound up with an ant farm consolation prize. She returned to the bleachers and sat down next to me, clutching the ant farm close to her chest. I shot arrows out of my eyes at her, but she didn't seem to notice.

How could my best friend do this to me? She took all my work and effort (not to mention the ant farm that was rightfully mine), and she didn't have to do bupkis.

As an adult I coined the phrase, "The Bozo Effect" for this phenomenon of a friend or co-worker getting the glory while someone else did all the work. Linda's lucky I didn't call it, "The Ligrano Effect."

If You Are You, Then Who Am I?

I met Doug in the summer before my senior year at UCLA. I was working full time for the summer at the Getty Museum as a docent for the French furniture collection, and when I wasn't docenting I was guarding ("Please don't touch that"). My boyfriend (and future husband) and I had recently split up, because I wanted some sort of commitment and he wasn't ready to commit to our future.

At the Getty I worked with a young married couple, Ann and Paul, who were everyone's favorites. I thought of them as the prince and princess of the museum. Paul was tall, blond, and very lean and Swedish-y, with a goatee that did not present as pretentious on his face. Ann was tall, lean, and beautiful, with Susan Sarandon-y russet hair and blue eyes. Both of them were in graduate school and were older and wiser. Oh, and did I mention that they were SO DAMN NICE??? Yes, they were so damn nice.

I wanted to be Ann. Hell, I wanted to be Paul. You can imagine my delight when, one day, out of the blue, they casually asked me if I wanted to meet a friend of theirs who was out for the summer, studying political science for some reason or another, at USC. OK, I will admit the USC part didn't sit well (UCLA Bruins will understand), but I decided, hell, I have no social life, my mother is dead, I hate my father, so why not.

Paul, Ann, and Doug picked me up at home and we went to see the movie version of Fiddler on the Roof, which I thought was a strange choice because Ann and Paul were not Jewish, and I had no idea about Doug. We had a nice time, the movie was long, it was sad, and I kept watching Doug to see if he identified with the story. Nothing.

A few days later, Doug called and asked for a date, just the two of us.

He was living near UCLA, so I picked him up and we went to a free concert in the rotunda of the library across from Royce Hall. It was the student chamber orchestra playing some Bach Brandenburg Concertos. OK so far. Then we decided to go to Doug's place and watch the TV rerun of the UCLA basketball game.

Doug had rented a small apartment on Weyburn in a complex that sported a Spanish tile roof, lots of arches, and a central garden with a fountain. Doug's place was in the basement, with the windows that only showed people's feet as they walked by. I get it, you shouldn't judge people by their windows.

After some preliminary talk, we settled in on his futon to watch the game. Doug put a few moves on me, very nice, very gentle, and I kind of enjoyed kissing him. It didn't go beyond kissing and a little touching, but that's all I wanted, certainly on a sort-of-first date.

The game ended, Doug walked me to my car, we kissed and Doug said he would call. He said it in a way that made me feel I had passed some test and he was definitely interested.

For the next few days, I rushed to answer the phone. No Doug. After a week, there were….crickets. At the Getty, Ann asked me how things had gone with Doug. I casually replied that I liked him and actually thanked her for setting the two of us up.

A month later, Paul mentioned that it was too bad Doug had to go home (to Maryland?). I was all, "Oh yeah, too bad, well, who knows….etc etc etc." Inside I was dying. Doug never called, and then just left.

All I could think was, "I must not have been good enough for him, I didn't go far enough for him, he didn't like something about me," blah, blah, blah. My self-confidence, already shaky from my boyfriend breakup, dipped to a point that it hardly registered on the "Love Who You Are" scale. I felt ashamed, humiliated, and deep down I felt angry, really angry.

It was all about how deficient I was. Nothing about Doug.

Looking back at it today, I know that Doug had some 'splaining to do. It was never about me, I just didn't know it at the time. To quote the classic song Chain of Fools, "You treated me mean, babe, oh yeah you treated me cruel."

Are you wondering if I ever looked Doug up on Facebook? OF COURSE I looked him up, probably a year ago. First off, I was amazed I even remembered his full name. And there was only one of him (naturally), and there he was, all white hair and paunch (meow). He had had an exclusive career at the Department of Defense (remember the poli-sci), and I instantly knew he was not the one for me.

Plus I look WAY better than his wife (you know I had to say that).

Forgetting To Feed

My sense of time has become capricious. Maybe it's because I'm not in an office anymore, and schedules and meetings don't have the cachet they once had. I know what day of the week it is, although lately I find myself saying, "I know it's Thursday, but it feels like Sunday."

I used to pay bills on time or early, and the concept of a library book past its due date was enough to produce palpitations. No more, and it's both liberating and disconcerting at the same time. Hell, my teachers noted my dependable nature and praised me for it. Dependable, good girl, always on time, always prepared, always offering to set up, always staying late on Thanksgiving to clean up. You get the picture.

I can't tell you when my slide into temporal delinquency began, but it's been a steady progression. Recently I returned a library book with a $3.20 overdue fine. I didn't break out in a sweat, I just handed the gal at the desk a fiver, got my change, and walked out. What's wrong with me?

I promised to send a friend an email with a link to non-toxic makeup, and promptly forgot. I promised myself that I would absolutely mail off that birthday card. Didn't happen.

There was even one time when, at 10:30pm I walked into the kitchen and saw the dog's bowls on the kitchen counter, and the dogs lying on the floor, waiting patiently. That was the first (and hopefully last) time I ever forget to feed them.

It's worrying, but it doesn't feel like dementia. It feels like "overwhelmia." I just made that up, but you get the drift. There is just too much information, too much overload, too many Facebook entries, too many fascinating links, too much social media, too many technical gadgets to learn, update, and troubleshoot, too much anger, too many idiots, too much stress, too many misunderstandings, and too much blah blah blah.

I don't much care what others think of me, but I'd still like to stay in my dogs' good graces.

Invisible

Invisibility might be a great superpower for a man, but for a woman it's just a "meh."

I've been trained my whole life to be invisible. As a child I was quiet, reserved, and obedient. I was taught to obey parents, teachers, religious leaders, and by extension any other adult I encountered. Salespeople and cashiers at the local Thrifty's terrified me. I was afraid they would see me doing something forbidden, like thumbing through the comics, and report me to the police, and my parents would have to bail me out and lose faith in my goodness.

As I approached puberty, our culture taught me to be a "lady" and always keep my legs together, speak softly, and don't compete with the boys, lest they think you were smarter and therefore not dating material. Demure was highly preferable to opinionated.

The sexually attractive years were a confusing time of visibility and invisibility. Walking down the street could invite unwanted catcalls, but they weren't personal; I felt stripped bare and anonymous at the same time.

As a software engineer, less qualified men got promoted and praised at work, and my ideas somehow became my male colleague's brilliant ideas. As a supervisor one time I stood up to another supervisor's dismissive treatment and was called into my (male) manager's office to explain MY offensive behavior.

And now, in my "wisdom years," I walk down the street as invisible as dandelion fluff in the breeze.

I decided it was time to change. Now I am likely to make myself heard at the store, the post office, Trader Joe's, resolving billing issues, hiring workers for the house, and in any other situation I want. This week I went to a new improv class and discovered I am the only woman. I asked questions, made witty remarks, and teased the other students to get them off their game, so they would see me in a different light, as someone to be reckoned with.

It felt damn good. I've come a long way, baby.

My Favorite Song

The year is 1970. I am a junior at UCLA studying art history and working part-time at the Getty Museum in Malibu. My mother has been sick for a year. She has had surgery, and many doctors' appointments and blood tests. She tells me she has a problem with her blood, that's all. I wait for her white cell count results over and over, celebrating when it moves up a notch, and worrying when it doesn't. She still works at her sales job, and life goes on.

I am aware she is sick, but she never complains and hardly talks about it at all. I know something is not right but I cannot bring myself to confront her. I don't really want to know, anyway. I have to study and take tests and go to work and maybe go out with my boyfriend sometimes. He's not a steady boyfriend, but we knew each other in high school and I enjoy his company.

I'm scared. No one in the family talks. Something is wrong.

I go through the day, taking care of business. I study. I work. I eat dinner. I watch TV.

One Saturday evening I am at my girlfriend's dorm on campus. I pass by an open door and hear a song that haunts me. The words, the singer's voice, so personal, like he is singing to me.

I have never heard this singer before. Strange name. Elton John. "Your Song."

It's a little bit funny this feeling inside
I'm not one of those who can easily hide
I don't have much money but boy if I did
I'd buy a big house where we both could live
If I was a sculptor, but then again, no

Or a man who makes potions in a travelling show
I know it's not much but it's the best I can do
My gift is my song and this one's for you
And you can tell everybody this is your song
It may be quite simple but now that it's done
I hope you don't mind
I hope you don't mind that I put down in words
How wonderful life is while you're in the world

If only someone felt that way about me. Someone who cherishes me, wants to support me. Wouldn't that be nice.

The year is 1971. My mother dies of leukemia. I never get a formal diagnosis until someone tells me, two days before, that she is dying.

Life goes on, they say. Sure, in a stupor of grief.

I am driving to school one morning, on Santa Monica Boulevard near Wilshire, and a song comes on the radio. Simon and Garfunkel's latest.

When you're weary, feeling small
When tears are in your eyes, I'll dry them all (all)
I'm on your side, oh, when times get rough
And friends just can't be found
Like a bridge over troubled water
I will lay me down
Like a bridge over troubled water
I will lay me down

I drive through the tears.

These Shoes Felt Great In The Store, But Now...

I met Michelle a few months after I retired from the corporate world. I still wanted to work, maybe do some consulting or IT projects or technical writing to keep my hand in the game. Michelle and her partner owned a contract consulting firm, and I met her through my good friend, who had met Michelle at a Chamber of Commerce mixer.

I did some consulting gigs, and over time Michelle and I became friendly, then close friends. She was also a ceramic artist and helped me choose a ceramic kiln, clay, and glazes for my mosaic work. We stayed at her cabin in Lake Arrowhead. She recommended her vet for our dogs. She lived a few blocks away, and sometimes my husband and I would go over for dinner.

I considered Michelle a good friend, yet I did not know very much about her. She rarely talked about her family, and I had a sense that there were parts of her life that would never open to me. It wasn't ideal, but all of the other aspects of our friendship were so pleasant that I let it go. Nobody's perfect, I thought.

About two years into our friendship, things began to change. Michelle stopped calling, stopped suggesting we get together. I kept calling, she would sound receptive, we would even agree to an event, and then the day of the event, nothing, a no-show with no call. Once she called the next day to say she had slept late and so missed our appointment. This went on until there was no contact at all.

After three months of this stop-and-go, I decided I wanted to keep our friendship; I missed her. I mailed her a card that said, "I miss you, and I hope you will be my friend again." Simple, to the point. Two weeks later she called, and we resumed the same pattern of making dates and then her not showing up and not letting me know.

Weeks passed. I made one final effort to repair the friendship. I wrote her and said I didn't understand the dynamic but I was willing to work together to bring the good times back. She replied that "I am who I am", take it or leave it.

I left it.

My only regret is that I tried to resurrect a relationship that didn't really exist in the first place, and I should have realized it sooner. I wanted to believe, so I believed.

The Inevitability Of Red Sauce

After experiencing a sad and frustrating social life in high school, I couldn't wait to graduate and go to college, where I planned to disappear and then rise, like the phoenix, from the ashes of teenage angst and recreate myself in a new persona. I would be successful, make new friends, exude confidence, and go into the future with my head held high. UCLA, here I come!

I met Regina in an English class, and we became acquaintances, then friends. Reggie was smart and perky. She played the viola and planned to be a music teacher; we bonded over our love of classical music. Reggie also belonged to a women's service club on campus, and she encouraged me to join so we could take part in activities together. Fine, sign me up.

UCLA put on an annual carnival, with a Ferris wheel, roller coaster, and bumper cars as the biggest attractions. There were food booths, of course. Our service club always manned (or womanned) the pizza booth. My boyfriend and I had planned to go to the carnival anyway, so I volunteered to work a shift making pizzas, and then spend the rest of the evening with my boyfriend.

I wanted a special outfit for the date, so I went to Ohrbach's where my mother worked and bought a rather risqué (for me) white see-through blouse, with opaque white circles sewn on at irregular intervals, so it gave the illusion of transparency. I felt rather chic and grown up, and couldn't wait to see my boyfriend's reaction.

The night of the carnival, I arrived for my two-hour shift and was schooled in the fine art of pizza-making: take the dough, pour on the red sauce, sprinkle the mozzarella cheese, and pop it in the oven. No problem, I thought, and I tackled my first pizza. It was a little sloppy, but as long as it tasted good, who cared?

I was getting pretty cocky about my pizza-making talents, and a half hour before my shift ended I lugged a full sauce container off the shelf, opened it, and started to pour when my foot hit a divot in the grass and a large plop of oily red sauce ended up on my pristine white blouse.

Oh fuck. I kept my cool, but inside I was in a freefall. I ran to the only water source I could think of, the porta potties, but there wasn't any water. Aaaaaaaggggggghhhhh! My boyfriend was due to pick me up in ten minutes. I went back to the booth, took some paper towels and tried to wipe the red-orange goo off, but I only succeeded in enlarging the stain. I started to feel hot, like I had a fever, a sure sign I was about to go into a panic attack. I talked myself down and waited for the inevitable.

My boyfriend came by the booth, looked at my blouse, and said nothing. I made a weak reference to my heart being so glad to see him that it was bursting onto my blouse, but inside I was dying.

We spent the rest of the evening at the carnival, but I couldn't wait to come home and take off that blouse, like Hester Prynne ripping off her scarlet letter. The stain got lighter with every wash, but it always retained a noticeable pink tint.

I never went back to the service club, and my friendship with Regina fizzled out.

Doing The Right Thing

The Time: When Dinosaurs Roamed the Earth
The Place: Laurel Elementary School Auditorium, West Hollywood, California
The Event: Sixth Grade Graduation "Sock Hop"

I loved the auditorium. It represented the best times at school, the rehearsal space for chorus, performance space for concerts ("On the fifth day of Christmas, my true love sent to me..."), and the site of my literary triumph in fifth grade, reciting Joyce Kilmer's "Trees" to a packed, appreciative PTA audience, including a rare visitation from my mother and grandmother to school.

The afternoon of my graduation party, I entered the auditorium with a sense of excitement, and also trepidation: it was a "sock hop," I didn't know how to dance, and I was fat. The girls removed their black and white saddle shoes, placed them near the door, and joined the other girls in small groups, giggling and gossiping about the boys and daring them to dance. The boys were plastered against the walls, trying not to look too frightened.

Someone had decorated the ceiling and walls with colorful crepe paper streamers. The folding chairs were all put away, leaving a large, shiny wood floor for dancing. Chubby Checker tantalized us to twist the night away. I stayed by the door and watched.

In order to look busy, I went to the refreshments table and filled a Dixie cup with Hawaiian punch. Then I noticed the pizza. It was like something out of the movies: our eyes met and we were locked in a moment of pure desire, the pizza and me.

Pizza was a delicacy in our family. We rarely ate it, and when we did it was Ralph's frozen pizza, not fresh-made from the Piece O' Pizza on Beverly Boulevard. PTA moms were serving up slices on a small paper plate. I took one, and the Hawaiian punch, and stood around near the door.

Oh my god that pizza tasted wonderful. Pizza was my friend and personal savior.

I wanted another slice but my intuition alerted me that getting another piece would draw negative attention. I didn't care, the lure of the pizza was strong. So after a few minutes I returned to the table, and….what's this? God no…Mrs. Jonas was handing out the refreshments. NO!!!!!!

In the sixth grade I had the worst crush on Louis Jonas. He did not return my ardor, but gave me subtle hints that he might like me just a smidgeon, like calling me names and running away. So romantic. I had never met Mrs. Jonas but I knew who she was.

Decision time, crap, crap, crap. The call of the pizza was too primal, too strong. I walked up to the table with a swagger I did not feel, put my hand down, and just as I was about to take the paper plate filled with my prize, Mrs. Jonas's voice rang out in a voice loud enough for everyone to hear:

"OH HONEY, DO YOU REALLY NEED TO EAT A SECOND PIECE OF PIZZA?"

Please, Lord, let the shiny wood floor open and swallow me up whole. My face turned into a beet, all the PTA moms were staring, and I wanted to die.

"Yes, I do need a second piece of pizza," I responded in a sure, confident, totally fraudulent voice.

I took that pizza to the doorway and ate it, but it tasted like sawdust. I found my shoes easily, since they were scuffed up and somewhat disreputable, put them on, and walked out of the auditorium with a fake smile plastered on my face.

That evening my mother asked how the dance had gone. I replied, "It was great…and they had pizza."

The Best Prescription

The best advice I ever received came from a totally unexpected source.

It was thirty months into my marriage. I was twenty-seven. We had relocated from Davis and were living in an apartment in the Palms area near West LA. My husband, who had passed the bar but was unable to find employment as a lawyer, had opened his own law firm in Marina del Rey, with two friends. In addition to being the bookkeeper for the firm, I had finally snagged a real job as assistant to the vice president of Norton Simon, Inc. in mid-Wilshire.

The law firm was going nowhere fast. His first client turned out to be a crazy man who wound up stalking us (I still remember his name). I had no experience as a bookkeeper and was totally winging it. I would come home from my real job and spend a few hours every night trying to make sense of the firm's accounting from the other two partners (and I use that term loosely).

Our marriage was in trouble. I was too young and naïve to understand that my husband had a serious addiction. He told me to keep our life private and to never talk about it to his parents. And I didn't. Not one word.

In fact, I didn't talk to anyone about my situation. I had gotten very good at keeping family secrets in my own family, so his request seemed pretty normal.

After we returned to LA from Davis, I asked my aunt to find a good general doctor in our area, just in case we needed medical attention. My aunt Sylvia, god bless her, was very resourceful, and had taken the bus to

Culver City and stood outside a medical office building, asking people who exited if they liked their doctor, and could she have his name please?

As the days wore on, my gut started to hurt, and my stress levels got so high I grew concerned about high blood pressure and a possible heart attack. One day, at work, things got so bad that I made a doctor's appointment and was able to see him immediately.

As I said, I did not know this doctor well. His office was very old-fashioned, with mismatched furniture and old table lamps on colonial maple tables. The rug in the waiting room was well-worn.

The nurse called me into the examining room. I put on the super-fashionable gown, sat on the metal table and waited.

Dr. Sloan entered, shook my hand, and sat down. He asked me why I was there, and I told him about the stress in a general way. He took my blood pressure, looked at me and said, "Absolutely normal."

"Impossible," I returned. "How can it be normal when I feel so bad?"

He looked at me and, in a kindly manner, said, "Mrs. Teller…what's really going on here?"

I started to cry, and told kindly Dr. Sloan all of the secrets I had sworn to protect.

After a brief pause, he said, "Well, if your husband is the cause of all of your medical problems, perhaps it would be good if you were no longer with him."

BOOM! Did he just say what I think he said? I had not thought things had developed to this critical state, but talking to the doctor crystallized just how bad things were.

"Dr. Sloan, are you giving me a prescription for a divorce?" I stammered.

"Well… yes, I am," he replied thoughtfully, as though it were a surprise to him, too.

Suddenly I felt a weight lift off me, and I knew in my heart of hearts what I had to do.

I drove home, yanked a suitcase out of my closet, filled it with whatever was handy, and prepared to leave.

My husband came home as I was opening the door with the suitcase.

"I'm leaving. I'll be at Sylvia's if you need to call."

That was it. I shut the door, went downstairs to the garage, got in my car, and left.

The Worst Thing A Parent Can Do

Hey boys and girls, let's have a go! What are some of the worst things parents can do? OK, OK, I see hands, I see your hands up, yes, I will get to everyone, who shall I pick first?
1) I couldn't ask for things. I don't know why, maybe I am bad. It has to be me. Oooooh, here's the May Company Christmas catalog. Look at all these amazing toys!!!!!! Want want want want want want want want oh yeah too bad not for me.
2) I couldn't get my father's attention. Hey Daddy Daddy see this incredible little toy car with the suction cup and the pull cord that ACTUALLY WALKS UP WALLS???? Look I'll show you how it works. Isn't that the coolest thing you've ever seen?? Huh?? Oh, OK, yeah, let's go.
3) I couldn't get a piano. I wanted a piano ever since I saw and heard one, what maybe three or four years old. I loved loved pianos and wanted one so badly I would have done anything to get one. Yes, anything. The neighbor's kid had a beat-up upright piano, sheet music, and a teacher, for God's sake. If I could have gotten away with it, I would have killed that unappreciative twit and moved that piano right into our (second floor) apartment.
4) I couldn't have a Ginny doll with her totally fab clothes and carrying case/closet with the nifty snap closure. Why do they have show-and-tell at school—to torture me? Sharon Levin, did you know you were torturing me that day when you showed your Ginny off to the class? Did you know how close you were to getting killed?
5) Mommy, you didn't tell me you were dying. What were you

thinking. Epic fail.
　You left me with Daddy. Epic-er fail.

Bullies All The Way Home

On the way:
Bully: Don't stop at Trader Joe's on your way home.
Me: I want to stop. I like Trader Joe's and I want a coffee sample. Maybe chocolate.
Bully: You have things to do at home.
Me: It can wait. I did a lot today. I want a diversion. Maybe chocolate.
Bully: Make it fast. No chocolate.

Arrival:
Me: Look at the pretty flowers. The stocks were Mommy's favorite. They smell so good.
Bully: People are looking at you. Don't smell the stocks.
Me: I ate my emergency Luna bar. I'll buy another one.
Bully: You know they aren't good for you. Too much sugar. Make a better choice.
Me: Look at all the different cheeses!
Bully: Cheese is fattening. Leave it alone.
Me: I haven't eaten chips for a long time. I deserve chips. I'll get the veggie chips, that's healthier.
Bully: Chips are poison. Remember to buy the toilet paper.
Me: I could have the smoked herring for lunch. Herring is full of healthy Omega-3's.
Bully: Smoked fish causes cancer.

Departure:
Checker: Did you find everything you wanted?

Me: Yes, thanks.

Arrival Home:
Bully: Put everything away. And clean the kitchen counters.
Me: OK.
Bully: Have a piece of fruit.
Me: I don't want a piece of fruit. I'm having that chocolate. Leave me alone.
Bully: Loser.

Poor Marks

I both looked forward to and dreaded going to my eleventh-grade Advanced American Lit class.

My teacher, Mr. Richard Battaglia, was matinee-idol handsome: tall, dark, and athletic, with lips that were recognizably sensual even to this innocent sixteen-year-old. When he strode down the highly-waxed floor to his classroom, all student traffic mysteriously evaporated; it was like Moses parting the Red Sea.

Mr. Battaglia wore black horn-rimmed glasses that perfectly matched his olive complexion and mahogany-flecked hair. The girls were in awe of him, and the boys wanted to BE him.

But Mr. Battaglia was not perfect. He knew his power to charm, and used it. He had favorites, especially some of the prettier girls in class. He paid attention to his pets and ignored the rest of us. To be in Mr. Battaglia's inner circle meant you had arrived, and you were happy to sit at his feet and catch any morsels of attention he cared to throw your way.

I was well aware I was not one of "Battaglia's girls." Try as I might, I could not get his attention or please him. Even worse, one of his pets, Rochelle, had been my best friend but had recently decided to shun me for no particular reason, which made things even worse.

Although I didn't have the pretties, I was respected as a smart girl. Smart was my claim to fame.

Mr. Battaglia gave the class an assignment to choose an approved novel and discuss some esoteric aspect of its existence. I remember being confused by the assignment and hesitantly going to Mr. B for help.

He was no help. He decided to give me a novel and choose a research topic I didn't quite understand. He assigned Uncle Tom's Cabin with an abstract philosophical question that went beyond my sixteen-year-old knowledge bank. I was stuck but Mr. Battaglia shooed me off and I knew I was on my own.

I did the best I could, but I was uneasy about the book report. I didn't understand what he wanted from me, and I muddled through and finished. I turned it in with a sinking feeling in my stomach.

A few days later, Mr. Battaglia went down the class rows, passing out the graded reports to their rightful owners. He came over to me, gave me a bit of a smirk, and sailed the paper to my desk so that others could see my grade.

The bastard gave me a D+. I was used to getting A's and a smattering of B's in my student career. The humiliation and shame was intense. It traveled from my stomach up to my neck and face, which I'm sure turned beet red. I turned the paper over and tried not to make eye contact with anyone as I gathered my books and got up to go to the next class.

Walking home after school, I was still in shock. Thank god it was Friday and I would have two days to recover and put some distance between me and school, even though I lived only two blocks away.

I never told my parents about the grade. I never told ANYONE about my grade. Mr. Battaglia had shaken me to my core.

At that point I could not see into the future and realize that the D+ would be an outlier, that I would continue to get mostly A's, graduate with honors from UCLA and go on to live my life.

Mr. Battaglia, you could have been a spectacular mentor, but that would have required a giving spirit and a genuine passion to make a difference.

You looked the part; too bad you didn't act the part.

My Permanent Record

In my elementary school there were degrees of disciplinary action. First came calling out in class, where you would just be humiliated in situ, as it were, with the other kids looking on. Next came the "Go into the cloakroom and stay there until I tell you to come out" gambit. Following that was "Go out into the hallway and wait" strategy. For the hard core there was always the "Go to the principal's office and I'm calling your parents" minefield. But to me, by far the worst possible threat was (and I shiver even now) "This will go on your PERMANENT RECORD!"

Oh god, not the permanent record. It sounded so, well, permanent. As in, following you to the grave, and, who knows, maybe they would read your educational felonies aloud to the mourners as they lowered you into the ground.

Whatever it was (and it was never explained), it didn't sound like a good idea to soil your permanent record.

When I was in my 40s, someone told me that I could pay a nominal fee and receive my Los Angeles Unified School District official file—my permanent record! I filled out the application, mailed my check and waited. Several months later I received a goldenrod parcel from the District, containing all of my records.

I had no idea, but at the end of each semester, teachers were obviously required to comment on each child in the class, because here were comments from all of my teachers, on my own permanent record.

I couldn't wait to read what they wrote. What would they say? How would they encapsulate twenty weeks of experiencing me into a line or two? What stood out to them?

So, in the interest of full disclosure, here are their assessments. Hold your applause until the end, please:

Kindergarten: "Dependable; mature; good mathematician; sings well; reserved; works independently."

First Grade: "Mature-very capable. Industrious; good work habits; well adjusted."

Second Grade: "Quiet-thinks things out and expresses herself well. A good student. Very dependable. Reads way above grade level."

Third Grade: "Good in all work. Well liked. Capable, thoughtful, industrious child."

Fourth Grade: "Loves music and art. Has much inner resources. Very intelligent, works hard, very dependable."

Fifth Grade: "Charming child-good work. Good math student-also good in other academic subjects."

Sixth Grade: "Above average in all subjects. Excellent in all academic subjects; expands and shows much verbal wit in permissive environment, worked hard this semester and expressed much positive regard for school for first time; a most capable child who needs acceptance & liking to bring out her best."

WTF????

This kid is ready for Harvard, and the Miss America pageant for sure.

Who are they talking about? It couldn't be me, because that is NOT how I experienced school.

Well liked? I was the fat kid who got teased.

Charming child? You mean I was obedient?

Reserved? Works independently? Perhaps I was terrified?

Above average in all subjects? I must come from Lake Wobegon!

Really, people? I am left with so many questions, but the most important one is this:

Didn't you think it might be—oh somewhat nice—IF YOU TOLD ME????

This praise languished in my permanent record for decades. What good did it do anyone, especially me?

But I get the last laugh, because now I know, and I don't have to live in fear of my permanent record anymore.

I think I'll go out and be charmingly above average.

The Cat (Harley) and Frannie, in correct billing order according to Harley's attorney

About The Authors

Honestly, what else do you need to know about these three? They live in cities, with people—presumably family. You got the juicy bits already

Made in the USA
San Bernardino, CA
26 August 2019